PETERSON'S DIRECTORY OF COLLEGE ACCOMMODATIONS

PETERSON'S DIRECTORY OF COLLEGE ACCOMMODATIONS

The Low-Cost Alternative for Travelers in the United States and Canada

Jay Norman

Peterson's Guides
Princeton, New Jersey

Copyright © 1989 by Peterson's Guides, Inc.

All rights reserved. No part of this book may be reproduced, stored in a retrieval system, or transmitted, in any form or by any means—electronic, mechanical, photocopying, recording, or otherwise—except for citations of data for scholarly or reference purposes with full acknowledgment of title, edition, and publisher and written notification to Peterson's Guides prior to such use.

Library of Congress Cataloging-in-Publication Data

Norman, Jay, 1924–
  Peterson's directory of college
  accommodations : the low-cost alternative for
  travelers in the United States and Canada / Jay
  Norman.
    p.   cm.
  ISBN 0-87866-869-1
  1. Hotels, taverns, etc.—United States—
Directories.   2. Hotels, taverns, etc.—Canada—
Directories.   3. Dormitories—United States—
Directories.   4. Dormitories—Canada—
Directories.   I. Title.   II. Title: Directory of
college accommodations.
TX907.2.N67   1989
647.947301—dc20   89-39084
                                         CIP

Composition and design by Peterson's Guides

Front cover photograph courtesy of Smith College.

Back cover photograph copyright 1985 by Benjamin Ailes. Reproduced by permission.

Printed in the United States of America

10   9   8   7   6   5   4   3   2   1

CONTENTS

PREFACE xv

DIRECTORY OF COLLEGE ACCOMMODATIONS

United States

Alabama
Talladega
  Talladega College 2
Tuskegee
  Tuskegee University 2

Alaska
Anchorage
  Alaska Pacific University 4
Sitka
  Sheldon Jackson College 4

California
Arcata
  Humboldt State University 7
Davis
  University of California, Davis 7
Hollywood
  Hollywood International Center (Y) 8
Los Angeles
  The Clark Hotel 9
  University of Southern California 9
Oakland
  Mills College 10
Palo Alto
  Stanford University 11
San Francisco
  San Francisco Central Y 12
  San Francisco State University 12
Santa Cruz
  University of California, Santa Cruz 13

Colorado
Denver
  Loretto Heights College 15
  Regis College 15

College Accommodations

Pueblo
    University of Southern Colorado 15

Connecticut
Stamford
    Stamford YMCA 17
West Hartford
    University of Hartford 17

District of Columbia
    Catholic University of America 19
    Gallaudet University 20
    The Harrington 20

Florida
De Land
    Stetson University 22
Lake Wales
    Warner Southern College 22

Georgia
Milledgeville
    Georgia College 24

Hawaii
Honolulu
    University of Hawaii at Manoa 25
Laie
    Brigham Young University–Hawaii 26

Idaho
Caldwell
    College of Idaho 28

Illinois
Chicago
    DePaul University 30
De Kalb
    Northern Illinois University 31
Quincy
    Quincy College 31
Waukegan
    Shimer College 32

Indiana
Upland
    Taylor University 34

Iowa
Indianola
    Simpson College 35

Contents

Le Mars
    Westmar College 35

Kansas
McPherson
    Central College 37
Wichita
    Kansas Newman College 37

Kentucky
Lexington
    Transylvania University 39

Louisiana
New Orleans
    International Center Y 42
    Loyola University 42
    Tulane University 42

Maine
Brunswick
    Bowdoin College 44

Maryland
Baltimore
    College of Notre Dame of Maryland 45
Lanham
    Washington Bible College 46
Takoma Park
    Columbia Union College 46

Massachusetts
Amherst
    University of Massachusetts at Amherst 47
Boston
    Boston Central Y 49
    Garden Halls Dormitories 49
    North East Residence Hall 49
Fitchburg
    Fitchburg State College 50
Waltham
    Bentley College 50

Michigan
Detroit
    Mercy College of Detroit 52
Grand Rapids
    Calvin College 52

College Accommodations

Midland
    Northwood Institute 53
University Center
    Saginaw Valley State University 54
Ypsilanti
    Eastern Michigan University 54

Minnesota
Bemidji
    Bemidji State University 56
Collegeville
    Saint John's University 56
Duluth
    College of St. Scholastica 56
Mankato
    Mankato State University 57
Marshall
    Southwest State University 58
St. Paul
    College of St. Catherine 58
Waseca
    University of Minnesota Technical College,
        Waseca 59

Mississippi
Holly Springs
    Rust College 61
Tougaloo
    Tougaloo College 61

Missouri
Jefferson City
    Lincoln University 63
Joplin
    Missouri Southern State College 63
Kansas City
    Rockhurst College 64
Parkville
    Park College 64
St. Charles
    Lindenwood College 65
St. Louis
    Washington University 65

Montana
Billings
    Eastern Montana College 67

Butte
    Montana College of Mineral Science and
        Technology 67

Nebraska
Blair
    Dana College 68
Omaha
    Omaha Y 69
Peru
    Peru State College 69
Seward
    Concordia Teachers College 70

New Hampshire
Rindge
    Franklin Pierce College 72

New Jersey
Princeton
    Westminster Choir College 74

New Mexico
Santa Fe
    College of Santa Fe 76

New York
Albany
    State University of New York at Albany 77
Bronx
    Fordham University 78
Buffalo
    Canisius College 78
Delhi
    State University of New York College of
        Technology at Delhi 79
Houghton
    Houghton College 79
New York
    Fashion Institute of Technology 80
    Union Theological Seminary 81
    YMCAs
        McBurney Y 82
        Vanderbilt Y 82
        West Side Y 82
        William Sloane House Y 82
Purchase
    Manhattanville College 82

College Accommodations

Staten Island
    Wagner College 83

North Carolina
Chapel Hill
    University of North Carolina at Chapel Hill 84
Greensboro
    Greensboro College 85

North Dakota
Valley City
    Valley City State University 86
Wahpeton
    North Dakota State College of Science 87

Ohio
Athens
    Ohio University 89
Cincinnati
    College of Mount St. Joseph 90
    University of Cincinnati 90
Hiram
    Hiram College 90
Steubenville
    Franciscan University of Steubenville 91
Toledo
    University of Toledo 91

Oklahoma
Tahlequah
    Northeastern State University 93

Oregon
Portland
    Warner Pacific College 94

Pennsylvania
Cresson
    Mount Aloysius Junior College 96
Greensburg
    Seton Hill College 96
Philadelphia
    La Salle University 97
Pittsburgh
    Carlow College 98
    Point Park College 99
Slippery Rock
    Slippery Rock University of Pennsylvania 99

South Dakota
Aberdeen
>Northern State College 100

Rapid City
>National College 101

Tennessee
Knoxville
>University of Tennessee, Knoxville 102

Murfreesboro
>Middle Tennessee State University 103

Nashville
>Fisk University 103

Texas
Arlington
>Bauder Fashion College 105

Denton
>Texas Woman's University 105

El Paso
>University of Texas at El Paso 106

Huntsville
>Sam Houston State University 107

San Antonio
>Bullis House 108
>St. Mary's University of San Antonio 108

Vermont
Johnson
>Johnson State College 110

Rutland
>College of St. Joseph 110

Virginia
Alexandria
>Alexandria/Washington Y 112

Arlington
>Marymount University 112

Charlottesville
>University of Virginia 113

Ferrum
>Ferrum College 113

Harrisonburg
>Eastern Mennonite College 114

Lynchburg
>Liberty University 114

College Accommodations

Sweet Briar
    Sweet Briar College 114

Washington
Cheney
    Eastern Washington University 116
College Place
    Walla Walla College 116
Seattle
    Seattle Downtown YMCA 117

West Virginia
Huntington
    Marshall University 118
Montgomery
    West Virginia Institute of Technology 119
Morgantown
    West Virginia University 120
Salem
    Salem College 120
Wheeling
    Wheeling Jesuit College 120

Wisconsin
La Crosse
    Viterbo College 122
Oshkosh
    University of Wisconsin–Oshkosh 123
Platteville
    University of Wisconsin–Platteville 124
Williams Bay
    George Williams College, Lake Geneva
        Campus 124

Canada

Alberta
Calgary
    University of Calgary 127
Edmonton
    University of Alberta 128
Fairview
    Fairview College 129

British Columbia
Burnaby
    Simon Fraser University 131

Vancouver
University of British Columbia 131
Victoria
University of Victoria 132

Manitoba
Winnipeg
University of Manitoba 134

New Brunswick
Fredericton
University of New Brunswick 135

Newfoundland
St. John's
Memorial University of Newfoundland 137

Nova Scotia
Antigonish
St. Francis Xavier University 139
Church Point
Université Sainte-Anne................. 139
Halifax
Dalhousie University 140
Mount Saint Vincent University 140

Ontario
Guelph
University of Guelph 141
London
University of Western Ontario 142
North York
York University 143
Ottawa
Carleton University 143
St. Catharines
Brock University 144
Thunder Bay
Confederation College 144
Toronto
University of Toronto 145
Waterloo
University of Waterloo 146
Wilfrid Laurier University 146
Windsor
University of Windsor 147

College Accommodations

Prince Edward Island
Charlottetown
    University of Prince Edward Island 148

Quebec
Montreal
    McGill University 149
    Université de Montréal 150
Quebec
    Université Laval 151
Trois-Rivières
    Université du Québec à Trois-Rivières 151

Saskatchewan
Regina
    University of Regina 154

PREFACE

My wife and I have found that life together is a series of compromises, and one of the areas requiring the most compromise on my part has involved her insistence, when we travel, on the comforts of a Hilton or similar hotel, while I would prefer local flavor and color. In an attempt to be fair, periodically my wife would yield to my demands that we try a small hotel or attractive guest house, but all too often the local color turned out to include lumpy beds, insufficient hot water, paper-thin walls, a freeway outside the window, and other unappealing features.

While working our way home from Vancouver one summer, we stopped for dinner in a college town with a restaurant of some repute. It was a hot, muggy day, and the campus, with its spacious lawns and large shade trees, beckoned. We met some students who invited us to share their iced watermelon as well as their conversation, and we learned we could spend the night on campus for $6 each. This was real local color, and we grabbed it.

Entering the dorm was a trip back to the days of our youth. Our room was rather spartan, but was clean, comfortable, and, once we closed the door, quiet—students do study. While the bathrooms were down the hall, there was lots of hot water for luxurious showers. A bit of poking about revealed free laundry facilities in the basement, as well as kitchenettes on each floor. We also discovered the cafeteria, with a variety of edibles that made us forget we were no longer youngsters—we even tried the make-your-own sundaes!

We took an after-dinner stroll around the campus, sitting in porch swings and visiting with students and other guests, all of them eager to discuss the area's points of interest. Thanks to my wife's habit of taking notes, we ended up with a considerable list of museums, historic sites, and restaurants.

The place was so comfortable that we stayed several days, swimming in the campus pool, taking in a student musical, exploring the local craft shops, browsing through the library and art gallery, and generally having a super time.

Other guests had brought their children, who seemed to enjoy the "grown-up" experience of being on a college campus. We wished such facilities had been available when we'd been traveling with our kids.

That college campus opened a new world of alternative accommodations to us. By now, we've explored a number of campuses, and, without exception, they've been beautiful and comfortable. But we've also found that there is a shortage of information available to people like us who want to take advantage of these out-of-the-ordinary facilities. So we decided to collect our findings in this publication, furnishing only factual information as provided by the participating universities and colleges.

Please note that we have listed some colleges that cater only to groups. These are ideal for family get-togethers, since there is all the pleasure of visiting together and none of the extra housework. We have also included a few exceptions to college dorms: the family Ys in several major cities. They are available the year round and should be satisfactory to those who want to be in a city center.

In order to maintain their tax-exempt status, colleges sometimes require that members of the public have an educationally related purpose in order to use campus accommodations. However, looking over the campus for yourself, your children, or your grandchildren usually seems to be acceptable. Some colleges have kept prices the same for several years, while others have adjusted their charges frequently. In addition, other information can change. Always telephone ahead and ask to be connected to the housing or conference office. Unless otherwise noted, the rates given are per night.

What follows is the result of 2,500 questionnaires sent to universities and colleges in the United States and Canada. Not everyone replied, even though we know from personal experience that accommodations are available to the public at these institutions; we hope they will respond and be included in future editions.

If you want to travel in comfort and at relatively

low cost, give serious thought to college dorms throughout the United States and Canada.

Mill Valley, California
July 1989

DIRECTORY OF COLLEGE ACCOMMODATIONS

ALABAMA
The Camellia State
state flower: camellia; state bird: yellowhammer

Alabama, the twenty-second state, was admitted to the Union in 1819. It stretches from Tennessee in the north to a panhandle at Mobile on the Gulf of Mexico. Fishing and agriculture are its most important industries. While Montgomery is the state capital, Birmingham is the largest city, and Huntsville is the site of a major rocket-research facility. The terrain is mountainous in the northeast corner of the state, but rolling plains are the rule elsewhere. A drive through the countryside is rewarding.

Mobile, a major port city with a population of about 200,000, was founded by the French in 1701 and has at various times been a French, British, and Spanish possession. Of interest are its many antebellum mansions, the city hall, the 1842 Marine Hospital, and the cathedral. Today, Mobile is important for its shipbuilding, oil-refining, paper, textile, aluminum, and chemical industries.

Talladega College
Talladega, AL 35160

Rooms available: June and July
Rates: $15 single; $25 double
Facilities: Kitchenettes, laundry, shared bathrooms
Policy on children: Accepted
Notes: Small, friendly campus; only 500 students
Telephone: 205-362-0206

Established by the United Church of Christ in 1867, Talladega College is located on a 50-acre campus about 45 minutes from Birmingham.

Talladega, with a population of about 20,000, is one of the oldest towns in interior Alabama, and the home of the Alabama School for the Deaf and Blind. It is also the home of a motor speedway that features the Winston 500 NASCAR Grand National in May and the Talladega 500 Winston Grand National in August. Naturally, the Motorsports Hall of Fame is also in Talladega. Talladega National Forest and the Mount Cheaha resort area are nearby.

Tuskegee University
Tuskegee, AL 36088

Rooms available: All year
Rates: $23.40 single; $28.80 double
Facilities: Guest-house accommodations, cafeteria, snack bar, gym, private bathrooms
Telephone: 205-727-8011

Tuskegee University was founded in 1881 by Booker T. Washington as a black educational facility called the Tuskegee Normal and Industrial Institute. George Washington Carver conducted his famous agricultural experiments there, and the school is well known for its Carver Foundation and the Tuskegee Agricultural Research and Experimental Station. Located on a 5,000-acre campus in a rural area, Tuskegee University has been designated a National Historic Site.

The town of Tuskegee (population 11,000) was settled before 1763. It houses a veterans' hospital and antebellum mansions; a national forest is nearby.

ALASKA
The Last Frontier
state flower: forget-me-not; state bird: willow ptarmigan

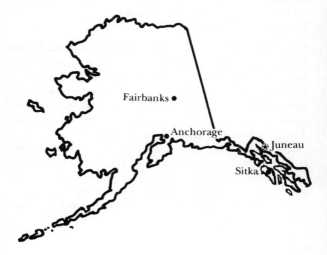

Alaska became a state in 1959; the largest in the Union, it's also the least populous. Its climate ranges from the subzero temperatures of the Arctic to the mild weather of the southern panhandle. Each area offers something different, and each is isolated from the others, maintaining contact by ship, radio, telephone, and air. The Alaska Highway runs inland and can't be used to reach interesting coastal towns.

The state capital is Juneau, while Anchorage is the major city. Aside from oil, which is carried by pipeline from Prudhoe Bay in the far north to Valdez, the ice-free port in the south, fishing is the state's main industry.

Alaska's glaciers are among the wonders of the world. Another unique sight is Mount McKinley, the highest mountain in the United States.

Alaska Pacific University
Anchorage, AK 99508

Rooms available: Third week in May to first week in August
Rates: $30 single; $20 double (3-day minimum stay)
Facilities: Cafeteria, laundry, pool, bike trails
Policy on children: Accepted
Restrictions: University prefers to cater to large groups
Notes: On bus line to downtown area; community plays available; view of the mountains
Telephone: 907-564-8248

Founded in 1959 as an independent institution, Alaska Pacific University is located on a 270-acre campus in a suburban area about a half mile outside of Anchorage.

Anchorage, a city of about 225,000, is the largest and most modern city in Alaska. It was established in 1914 and is the transportation and business center for south-central Alaska. Although Anchorage is quite large by Alaskan standards, it is still possible to pan for gold not far away, and there are a lake and recreation area close to the University. In addition, Anchorage offers several museums, a zoo, and original pioneer houses, as well as raft trips, helicopter tours, and hot-air balloon rides. Summer weather in the area is quite mild.

Sheldon Jackson College
Sitka, AK 99835

Rooms available: Throughout the year as space permits; heavily booked with groups
Rates: $20–$25 single; $15–$20 double

Facilities: Cafeteria on campus (meals $14 a day); also museum, library, fishery program, boat trips
Telephone: 907-747-5220

Established in 1878 as a training school for Tlingit Indians, Sheldon Jackson College is the oldest educational institution in Alaska; it is a private school associated with the United Presbyterian Church. The 345-acre campus, with its chalet-style buildings, is located in the town of Sitka on Baranof Island in southeastern Alaska's Alexander archipelago, about 100 miles from Juneau. It offers a view of the Pacific Ocean and a quiet sweep of small islands and forested mountains. Historic sites, parks, forest trails, tideland flats, and an Indian and Russian trading post are among the attractions. A famous collection of Native Alaskan artifacts is housed at the Sheldon Jackson Museum. A visitor center, the Russian Orthodox Cathedral of St. Michael, the Russian bishop's house, and the Centennial Building are situated near the campus.

Founded in 1799 by Aleksandr Baranov, Sitka was the territory's capital until 1900. The United States purchased Alaska from Russia in 1867, and an Alaska Day festival is held every October to commemorate the event. Fishing—for salmon, halibut, red snapper, herring, crab, abalone, and clams—remains Sitka's first industry, but there are also canning, processing, and lumber enterprises. In fact, the state logging championships are held here in July.

CALIFORNIA
The Golden State
state flower: golden poppy; state bird: California valley quail

The thirty-first state, California was admitted to the Union in 1850; its capital, Sacramento, in the heart of one of several agricultural valleys, is a port for oceangoing vessels! A leader in agriculture and industry, California has a mild climate that has attracted millions. Its diversity—from the redwood forests and mountain resorts of the north to the deserts of Death Valley and Palm Springs in the south, from the movies and glitter of Hollywood and Los Angeles to the cosmopolitan seaports of San Francisco and San Diego—offers so much of interest that the state almost defies classification.

Humboldt State University
Arcata, CA 95521

Rooms available: June 1 to mid-August (reservations required)
Rates: $28–$34, including meals
Facilities: Cafeteria, laundry, kitchenettes, shared bathrooms, store, gym, pool, theater
Policy on children: Accepted
Notes: Residence halls nestle in the redwoods 1 mile from Pacific Ocean
Telephone: 707-826-3451

Humboldt State University, founded in 1913, is the northernmost campus of the California State University System. The 142-acre campus, located in the town of Arcata, 275 miles north of San Francisco, is rural in atmosphere.

Arcata is on the Pacific Ocean; it is part of the Redwood Empire and is a lumber and fishing center. Nearby are Redwood National Park, Redwood State Park, and the Hoopa Valley Indian Reservation, as well as wild rivers for rafting and fishing, lumber mills, and Humboldt Bay itself.

University of California, Davis
Davis, CA 95616

Rooms available: All year
Rates: $42, including breakfast
Facilities: Cafeteria, sports facilities
Policy on children: Accepted
Restrictions: Visitors are required to have an educationally related purpose
Telephone: 916-752-8000

The University of California, Davis, part of the publicly supported University of California System, was established in 1906. Davis, which is primarily a university town, is noted for its fine bike paths and mandatory solar heating. The school is an agricultural and wine research center; the wine country of the Napa Valley is an hour's drive away.

Sacramento, the state capital, is only a few miles from Davis; among its attractions are the old Governor's Mansion, now a museum; Sutter's Fort; the Crocker Art Museum; Old Sacramento, a restored area offering shops, restaurants, and an annual jazz festival; and the Railroad

University of California, Davis (continued)
Museum. The California State Fair is a major event each Labor Day. The mountain resorts of Lake Tahoe are within a 2-hour drive by excellent freeway.

Hollywood International Center (Y)
1553 North Hudson
Hollywood, CA 90028

Rooms available: All year
Rates: $27 single; $37 double
Facilities: Cafeteria, shared bathrooms, fitness center, swimming pool
Policy on children: Accepted
Notes: Three- and 6-day tours of area available at reasonable rates
Telephone: 213-467-4161

Somehow Hollywood has a life of its own, even though it is part of Los Angeles. Known as the home of the movies, the area is famous for Graumann's (now Mann's) Chinese theater and its forecourt with the footprints of the stars.

LOS ANGELES

Incorporated in 1850, Los Angeles is the third-largest city in the United States. Two mountain ranges, the Santa Monica and Verdugo, cut through the city. The LA megalopolis covers 34,000 square miles and supports more than 10 million people, encompassing numerous coastal and inland cities. An extensive freeway system connects the various communities, but there is no comprehensive public transit system.

Los Angeles was the capital of the Spanish province of Alta California; it was also a cattle center under both Spanish and Mexican rule. The discovery of oil, the expansion of the railroad, and the flourishing of the movie industry in the early twentieth century began the area's dramatic growth. More recently, radio, TV, and general manufacturing have kept the boom going.

There are countless things to do and see around Los Angeles. Among the most popular are the amusement parks of Disneyland and Knott's Berry Farm; Universal Studios and several major television studios; the *Queen Mary* and *Spruce Goose;* and the Botanical Gardens. Ethnic Mexican, Chinese, Japanese, Indian, Korean, and Vietnamese neighborhoods and restaurants are of interest, as are a variety of museums containing works of art, scientific and industrial artifacts, and the bones of prehistoric animals recovered from the La Brea tar pits. Parks, racetracks, and beaches add to the attractions of the area.

The Clark Hotel
426 South Hill Street
Los Angeles, CA 90013

Rooms available: All year
Rates: $23–$37 single; $28–$42 double, depending on type of room
Facilities: Cafeteria, private baths available
Policy on children: Accepted
Notes: Package tours of from 3 to 6 days available at reasonable prices through the Y
Telephone: 213-624-4121

This hotel is operated by the local YMCA. It is located within walking distance of department stores, restaurants, the Music Center, the Museum of Contemporary Art, Little Tokyo, Chinatown, and Oliviera Street, with its Mexican-style ambience.

University of Southern California
Los Angeles, CA 90007

Rooms available: End of May to third week in August
Rates: $25 single; $17 per person, double
Facilities: Cafeteria; store; shared bathrooms; tennis, volleyball, and basketball courts

University of Southern California (continued)
Policy on children: Accepted
Notes: Theater and shopping malls across the street
Telephone: 213-743-2022

Founded in 1880 on land donated by a Protestant, a Catholic, and a Jew, the University of Southern California is a private school whose alumni constitute a large proportion of the professional people of Los Angeles County.

The 150-acre campus is close to the downtown business area of the city. Campus attractions include the Allan Hancock Foundation, Heritage Hall, the Fisher Art Gallery, the Science and Industry Museum, and the Natural History Museum.

Mills College
Oakland, CA 94613

Rooms available: Early June to mid-August (reservations required)
Rates: $67 per person, including 3 meals and daily maid service
Facilities: Cafeteria, laundry, kitchenettes, store, both private and shared bathrooms, swimming, tennis, jogging, campus theater
Policy on children: Accepted
Telephone: 415-430-2145

Mills College, founded in 1825, is an independent liberal arts school for women. Located on 128 wooded acres on the outskirts of Oakland, 25 minutes from San Francisco and 12 from Berkeley, it is convenient to the many attractions of the Bay Area.

Oakland, a city of 360,000 on the eastern shore of San Francisco Bay, is a shipping port and major rail terminus; among its industries are chemical and food-processing plants and glassworks. The city is the hub of the Bay Area Rapid Transit (BART) district, a model three-county public transit system. Oakland also has an international airport.

Of particular interest are the Oakland Museum, Chabot Observatory, and the rose gardens. Jack London Square, a waterfront dining and shopping area, is located on the Oakland estuary. The city is home to a symphony orchestra, fine parks, a state arboretum, a children's amusement park, a zoo, and a lovely lake.

California

Stanford University
Palo Alto, CA 94305

Rooms available: Mid-June to mid-September
Rates: $26.75 single; $19.75 per person, double
Facilities: Cafeteria, laundry, kitchenettes, store, shared bathrooms, swimming, tennis, golf
Policy on children: Those under 18 must be accompanied by an adult
Telephone: 415-723-3127

Stanford, founded in 1885, is a privately endowed university on 8,000 tree-covered acres. Specializing in research, much of it medical, Stanford is known particularly for the Stanford Research Institute; the Hoover Institute on War, Revolution, and Peace; and excellent museums of zoology and entomology. The Rodin Sculpture Garden adjoins the Stanford Art Museum. Also of interest are Memorial Church, Hoover Tower, and the Stanford Linear Accelerator Center.

The University is situated in the residential community of Palo Alto (south of San Francisco and north of San Jose), also known for its high-tech and publishing firms. Highway 280, one of the most scenic freeways in the state, connects Palo Alto to San Francisco.

SAN FRANCISCO

Founded in 1776, San Francisco is a major center of trade with the Orient and the financial and scenic hub of the Bay Area. Located at the end of a peninsula separating the Pacific Ocean from the bay, the picturesque city is built on steep hills and offers views from many neighborhoods.

World-famous tourist attractions abound—the cable cars, Golden Gate Bridge, Fisherman's Wharf, Chinatown, Golden Gate Park, Telegraph Hill, and the downtown stores—but San Francisco is also noted for its museums, symphony orchestra, opera and ballet companies, zoo, aquarium, planetarium, and restaurants serving the dishes of many countries. The Exploratorium, a hands-on science exposition, is popular with both children and adults. Also of interest are the international shopping bazaars of

San Francisco (continued)

Ghirardelli Square, the Cannery, Cost Plus, and Pier 39.

The attractive town of Sausalito, Muir Woods, and Mount Tamalpais are within easy driving distance to the north. Berkeley and Oakland are to the east, and San Jose and Silicon Valley to the south.

SAN JOSE

Founded in 1770, San Jose was the state capital from 1849 to 1851. Today, it's the heart of one of the fastest-growing areas in the state. Among its attractions are Marriott's Great America amusement park, the Winchester Mystery House, Alum Rock Park mineral springs, Kelly Park zoo and Japanese gardens, Rosicrucian Park with its planetarium and Egyptian and science museums, and Lick Observatory on nearby Mount Hamilton.

San Francisco Central Y
220 Golden Gate Avenue
San Francisco, CA 94102

Rooms available: All year
Rates: $24 single; $34 double (plus 11% tax)
Facilities: Fitness center, swimming pool, shared bathrooms
Policy on children: Accepted
Notes: Many excellent restaurants and fast-food outlets in the area
Telephone: 415-885-0460

This is an excellent location, within walking distance of the Civic Center, the Museum of Modern Art, Davies Symphony Hall, the opera, and the ballet.

San Francisco State University
San Francisco, CA 94132

Rooms available: June to mid-August (reservations advisable)

Rates: $35 single; $20 per person, double (3-day maximum stay)
Facilities: Cafeteria, laundry, store, shared bathrooms, tennis courts
Policy on children: Accepted
Notes: Rooms available to students, faculty, and staff of educationally related institutions
Telephone: 415-338-1067

San Francisco State University, established in 1899, is a publicly supported college. The 110-acre campus is located in the southwestern corner of the city, near the shores of Lake Merced. The school is known for its education and journalism departments and its theater productions. The University's location on the M line of the Muni Metro system gives it excellent access to the rest of the city. Stonestown, a major shopping center, is within walking distance of the campus.

University of California, Santa Cruz
Santa Cruz, CA 95064

Rooms available: Third week of June to third week of August
Rates: $45 (guest suite)
Facilities: Cafeteria
Policy on children: Not accepted
Telephone: 408-429-2611

The Santa Cruz campus of the University of California was established in 1965 on 2,000 acres of forest and meadowland. It is located about 75 miles from San Francisco, 35 miles from San Jose, and 45 miles from the picturesque coastal towns of Carmel and Monterey.

Santa Cruz itself is quite picturesque. Located on Monterey Bay, it has fine beaches, a municipal wharf dating from 1913 where name bands perform, and the Boardwalk, a venerable oceanside amusement park with one of the last wooden roller coasters in the country. Other attractions are the Roaring Camp Railroad, a marine laboratory, the Garden Project, and a replica of a 1791 Spanish mission.

COLORADO
The Centennial State
state flower: Rocky Mountain columbine; state bird: lark bunting

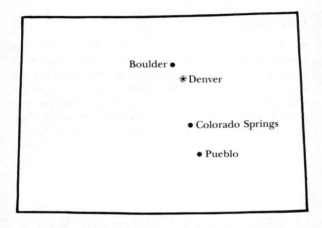

Colorado was admitted to the Union in 1876, thereby earning the nickname quoted above. Although its economy is based on minerals (molybdenum, coal, uranium, high-grade stone, and brick clay) and agriculture (potatoes, sugar beet, wheat, and flowers), tourism is a big contributor. The Rocky Mountains, eight national and many private parks, and the forests and recreation areas provide facilities for skiing, rafting, swimming, mountain climbing, boating, camping, hunting, and fishing.

Denver, the Mile-High City and state capital (population 600,000), has many parks and museums, a zoo, and a U.S. mint. Among Colorado's myriad scenic attractions are the Durango-Silverton steam train; Mesa Verde National Park, with the well-preserved cave dwellings of the Anasazi Indians; Rocky Mountain National Park, a wildlife sanctuary; the town of Ouray (Switzerland of the West); and the ski areas of Aspen, Vail, and Steamboat Springs.

Colorado

Loretto Heights College
Denver, CO 80236

Rooms available: Summer
Notes: This is a conference center operated during the summer for groups of 15 or more; call for rates
Telephone: 303-936-8841

Loretto Heights College was established in 1918 as a Roman Catholic school for women; it is now coeducational. The 105-acre campus is located at the foot of the Rocky Mountains in a suburban area 5 miles from downtown Denver.

Regis College
Denver, CO 80221

Rooms available: Second week in May to second week in August (reservations required)
Rates: $16–$20 single; $10–$16 per person, double
Facilities: Cafeteria, laundry, store, both private and shared bathrooms, basketball, racquetball, tennis, swimming, library, chapel, walking areas
Policy on children: Accepted, under adult supervision
Telephone: 303-458-3505

Regis College was founded in 1877 as a Catholic school under Jesuit direction. It has a 30-acre campus 4 miles from downtown Denver. Rocky Mountain National Park is 60 miles away, and Vail and Boulder are 100 and 30 miles away, respectively.

Denver is located on the South Platte River at an altitude of 5,280 feet. It is a processing and shipping center, and the financial and administrative center for the Rocky Mountain region. Its excellent transportation system and great beauty make tourism a leading industry.

University of Southern Colorado
Pueblo, CO 81001

Rooms available: June to first week in August
Rates: $7.50 per person, double

College Accommodations

University of Southern Colorado (continued)
Facilities: Cafeteria, shared bathrooms, tennis, volleyball
Policy on children: Accepted
Telephone: 719-549-2601

A state-supported institution, the University of Southern Colorado is located on an 800-acre campus about 2 miles from Pueblo.

Pueblo, a city of 100,000 incorporated in 1885, is the shipping, trade, and industrial center of an extensive coal, timber, livestock, and farming area. It is also the headquarters of San Isabel National Forest. Less than an hour's drive away is Colorado Springs, a beautiful resort city at the foot of Pikes Peak. In the Colorado Springs area, Garden of the Gods, a 950-acre natural park containing massive red-sandstone formations (particularly spectacular at sunrise and sunset); the Air Force Academy; Pikes Peak Ghost Town; and the U.S. Olympic Complex are all worth a visit.

CONNECTICUT
The Constitution State
state flower: mountain laurel; state bird: American robin

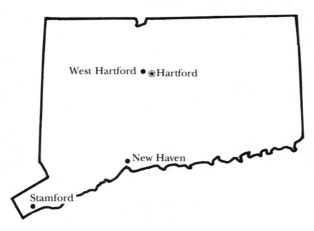

One of the original thirteen colonies, Connecticut was first settled in 1633 by Massachusetts residents moving to the area in order to escape the rigid religious requirements for citizenship set by the government of that state.

A manufacturing state but perhaps better known as the home of the headquarters of some fifty insurance companies, Connecticut is also famous for the shipyard at Groton, which turned out its first submarine in 1776.

In the capital, Hartford, is a plaque marking the site of the Charter Oak, where the state charter was hidden when the English governor demanded it be returned for cancellation. The boat-shaped headquarters of one of the city's insurance companies contains an insurance museum and art exhibits. The Harriet Beecher Stowe House is next door to Mark Twain's residence. Both authors were instrumental in establishing *The Hartford Courant,* the oldest newspaper in the nation.

The state has many historic sites. Among the most interesting is the old port and shipbuilding town of Mystic, which remains as it was in earlier days.

Stamford YMCA
909 Washington Boulevard
Stamford, CT 06103

Rooms available: All year
Rates: $24 single; $52 double
Facilities: Fitness center, swimming pool
Policy on children: Accepted
Telephone: 203-357-7000

The land that is now Stamford was bought from the Indians in 1640 and settled the next year. Stamford has a population of about 110,000. A research and manufacturing center, nevertheless it retains its charm as a New England maritime center.

There is a branch of New York's Whitney Museum of American Art in the city, as well as the Stamford Museum and Nature Center. In addition, the First Presbyterian Church is of interest for its architecture, abstract stained-glass windows, and carillon concerts.

University of Hartford
West Hartford, CT 06117

Rooms available: End of May to beginning of August (reservations required)

College Accommodations

University of Hartford (continued)
Rates: Variable (specifics on request)
Facilities: Cafeteria, laundry, kitchenettes, store, shared bathrooms, tennis courts, pool
Telephone: 203-243-4771

Located in West Hartford, a separate city with a population of approximately 62,000, the University was founded as the Hartford Art School in 1866. Subsequently, Hillyer College and the Hartt School of Music were merged with the Art School to form the University. Other schools have since been added, so that the present-day University consists of some thirty buildings on 200 acres.

West Hartford is the birthplace of Noah Webster of dictionary fame, and the house where he was born in 1758 is open to the public. Hartford is some 5 miles distant.

DISTRICT OF COLUMBIA
Justice for All
flower: American beauty rose; bird: wood thrush

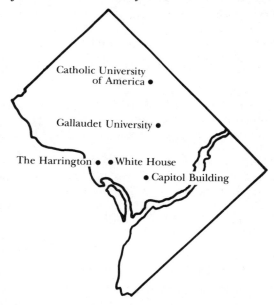

The District of Columbia, a 70-square-mile area in the state of Maryland, was established by Congress in 1790. Coextensive with the nation's capital, Washington, it is known to its 750,000 residents as The District.

Having one of the highest concentrations of historic, cultural, and scenic attractions in the world, the District of Columbia contains such sights as the White House; Constitution Hall; Ford's Theatre, where Abraham Lincoln was shot by John Wilkes Booth; the John F. Kennedy Center for the Performing Arts; the Library of Congress; the Lincoln Memorial; the National Air and Space Museum; the Smithsonian Institution; the Supreme Court Building; the Thomas Jefferson Memorial; the United States Capitol, with its two wings containing the Senate and House chambers; the U.S. National Arboretum and U.S. Botanic Garden; the Vietnam Veterans Memorial; the Washington Monument; and numerous museums, libraries, and galleries with such specialties as African art, the photographic work of Ansel Adams, armed forces artifacts, hands-on science exhibits for children, Jewish ceremonial art, Shakespearean manuscripts, firearms, natural history, the artistic achievements of women, and textiles. Other attractions include tours of Arlington National Cemetery and Mount Vernon. It is also possible to ride through Georgetown on the C&O Canal aboard a replica of a nineteenth-century mule-drawn canal boat.

Catholic University of America
Washington, DC 20064

Rooms available: End of May to early August
Rates: $16–$24 per person (3-day minimum stay)
Facilities: Cafeteria, laundry, kitchenettes, both semiprivate and shared bathrooms, lounges
Policy on children: Accepted, if accompanied by an adult
Note: Post office and subway stop on campus
Telephone: 202-635-5615

Catholic University of America, founded in 1887, is located on a 190-acre campus in a suburban area of Washington. Campus attractions include Hartke Theater and the National Shrine of the Immaculate Conception.

Mount Vernon, Baltimore's Harbor Place, and Old Town in Alexandria, Virginia, are all nearby.

College Accommodations

Gallaudet University
Washington, DC 20002

Rooms available: October–November, January–April
Rates: $20 per day (in advance), including room and board
Facilities: Cafeteria, shared bathrooms, swimming pool, gym, bowling alley
Policy on children: Not accepted
Restrictions: No cooking in rooms, no pets
Telephone: 202-651-5511, 800-672-6720

Founded in 1864, Gallaudet College is the world's only private liberal arts college for the deaf. The 97-acre campus is located in northeastern Washington.

The Harrington
E Street, NW, between 11th and 12th
Washington, DC 20004

Rooms available: All year
Rates: $38 single; $48 double
Facilities: Self-service cafeteria
Notes: All-inclusive package tours available at reasonable rates
Telephone: 202-628-8140

Located just four blocks from the White House, this hotel is within walking distance of many museums and historic sites, such as the Smithsonian Institution and the Mall area.

FLORIDA
The Sunshine State
state flower: orange blossom; state bird: mockingbird

Florida, admitted to the Union in 1845, is the most southerly of all the states. A long, low-lying peninsula, it is protected from the Atlantic Ocean on the east by many islands and sandbars. Among Florida's special features are the Everglades, 5,000 square miles of swampland; at the southwestern tip of the peninsula is Everglades National Park, the third-largest national park in the country. Naturally, beaches, swimming, skin diving, and sailing are great attractions here, but the state also offers Disney World, EPCOT Center, and Cape Kennedy, with its launchpads and space works.

A retirement haven, Florida is also vigorous and lively. Commercial fishing, citrus farming, lumbering, and other agricultural enterprises, including the sugarcane and melon crops planted on land reclaimed in a short-lived swamp-draining campaign, join tourism to support the economy. Port Everglades, 2 miles from Fort Lauderdale, is the home of many Caribbean-bound cruise ships.

Stetson University
De Land, FL 32720

Rooms available: Call for dates of availability
Rates: $10 per person
Restrictions: Minimum of 20 people; suitable for family reunions, social meetings, etc.
Telephone: 904-734-4121

Stetson University was founded in 1886 by Henry De Land, founder of the city of De Land. The University was founded with the help of John Stetson, of hat fame, and was named after him. The De Land Museum of Art in town and the Gillespie Museum of Minerals on campus are among the local attractions.

Warner Southern College
Lake Wales, FL 33853

Rooms available: Mid-May to mid-August
Rates: $12 per person
Facilities: Dorm-style accommodations, laundry, private bathrooms, tennis, basketball, racquetball
Notes: Golf course 5 minutes away; also nearby are Cypress Gardens, Disney World, Sea World
Telephone: 813-638-1426

Warner Southern is an independent, four-year, coeducational college, affiliated with the Church of God. Its 350-acre campus is in a rural setting, although there is easy access to Tampa.

Lake Wales, a town with a population of 8,500, is located in central Florida, southeast of Tampa. It is the winter base of the Black Hills Passion Play; performances are held in Lake Wales between mid-February and mid-April, after which it returns home to Spearfish, South Dakota, for the rest of the year. The town is also the locale of Spook Hill, where parked cars appear to roll uphill. Nearby are Bok Tower Gardens, with its daily carillon recitals and 128 acres of azaleas, camellias, magnolias, and gardenias, and the Lake Wales Museum and Cultural Center, housed in the former Seaboard Coast Line depot and containing exhibits on railroad and citrus history.

GEORGIA
Empire State of the South
state flower: Cherokee rose; state bird: brown thrasher

Georgia was established in 1733, the last of the original thirteen colonies. The state capital, Atlanta, is also the largest city; other important cities are Augusta, Savannah, Macon, Columbus, and Albany. Although the Sea Islands sit off the Atlantic coast and half the state is coastal plain, Georgia is best known for the Appalachian Plateau and the Blue Ridge Mountains. The state is drained by several major rivers, including the Savannah, which forms the border with South Carolina.

There is excellent saltwater fishing in the coastal channels and the surf of the Sea Islands, as well as freshwater fishing in the rivers. The resorts of the Sea Islands, Callaway Gardens at Pine Mountain, Lake Seminole, Lake Lanier, Stone Mountain Park, and the Chattahoochee and Oconee national forests provide diverse recreational opportunities. The wild and scenic Chattooga River, which runs through the Chattahoochee National Forest, offers rafting and canoeing. Okefenokee Swamp, in the southeast, is one of the largest swamps in the country and is famous for its wildlife.

Georgia College
Milledgeville, GA 31061

Rooms available: Third week in June to September 1
Rates: $7 per person
Facilities: Cafeteria, shared bathrooms, sports
Notes: The rooms are available primarily to those with educational purposes
Telephone: 912-453-5160

Georgia College was established in 1889 as a public institution. Its 45-acre campus is located in an urban area about 30 miles from Macon and 98 miles from Atlanta.

Milledgeville is a town of about 14,000 on the Oconee River in central Georgia. It was intended to be the state capital, and it served as such from 1807 to 1868. The 1807 capitol building and 1838 executive mansion are now on the grounds of the Georgia Military College. The area abounds in antebellum houses, Civil War monuments, and battle sites.

HAWAII
The Aloha State
state flower: hibiscus; state bird: Hawaiian goose

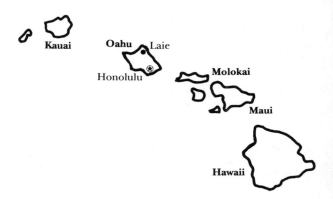

Hawaii, which became the fiftieth state in 1959, consists of eight major islands and many islets lying in a chain in the Pacific Ocean about 2,100 miles from the west coast of the mainland. Oahu, though it is the site of the state capital, Honolulu, and the most developed and populated of the islands, is not the largest. That honor goes to Hawaii.

The Hawaiian islands are volcanic in origin, and more than one volcano is still active, although the eruptions have not been particularly destructive of late. The islands are best known as paradisiacal resorts catering to mainlanders anxious to escape winter's rigors and the general stress of everyday life. Attractions range from the cosmopolitan pleasures of Honolulu to the unspoiled beauty of Kauai and the Big Island, Hawaii.

Of particular interest in Honolulu are Kapiolani Park, with its zoo and aquarium; the Waikiki Shell, where symphony concerts are held; the USS *Arizona* Memorial at Pearl Harbor: Bishop Museum; Iolani Palace; and Diamond Head.

University of Hawaii at Manoa
Honolulu, Oahu, HI 96822

Rooms available: Summer and winter Interim periods
Rates: $13.50 double, in dorms; $16 per person, in 4-per-

University of Hawaii at Manoa (continued)
    son apartments; $19.50 per person, in 2-person apartments

Facilities: Cafeteria, store, shared bathrooms, sports equipment, swimming pools, tennis courts, film and stage presentations
Policy on children: Accepted
Notes: Rooms available to groups
Telephone: 808-948-8177

Manoa is the principal campus of the University of Hawaii. It covers some 320 acres in the Manoa Valley and is part of a nine-campus system. There are a number of structures of note on campus, including Varney Circle, a palm-bordered fountain depicting a Hawaiian god; the Quadrangle, consisting of four of the original campus buildings; Andrews Outdoor Theater; and the courtyards and gardens of the Music Complex and Art Building.

Brigham Young University–Hawaii
Laie, Oahu, HI 96762

Rooms available: All year
Rates: $10 per person
Facilities: Cafeteria, sports equipment
Policy on children: Accepted
Restrictions: No smoking or drinking, no pets
Notes: Polynesian Cultural Center on campus, beaches nearby
Telephone: 808-293-3541

The Brigham Young University–Hawaii campus was founded in 1955 by the Mormon Church. The campus occupies 60 acres in an urban setting south of the Mormon Temple, about 40 miles north of Honolulu. The temple itself is well worth a visit.

    Laie is a tropical Pacific paradise, with its coral beaches, rolling surf, waterfalls, lush vegetation, and cloud-covered volcanic peaks.

IDAHO
The Gem State
state flower: syringa; state bird: mountain bluebird

Idaho became the forty-third state in 1890. The capital is Boise; Pocatello and Idaho Falls are other major cities. While cattle-raising, mining, and potatoes all contribute significantly to the economy, tourism is growing in importance. Rugged mountains, rushing rivers, spectacular gorges, and pristine wilderness are a magnet for adventurous hikers, white-water rafters, skiers, fishermen, hunters, and photographers. Hells Canyon is the nation's deepest gorge, the Snake and Salmon are two of its mightiest rivers, and the Rocky Mountains spread four ranges into the state. The northern panhandle contains the largest of Idaho's many lakes: Coeur d'Alene, Pend Oreille, and Priest. In sharp contrast is Craters of the Moon National Monument, 83 square miles of fantastic basaltic lava formations. The world-famous ski resort of Sun Valley is fast becoming a year-round vacation spot.

College of Idaho
Caldwell, ID 83605

Rooms available: June through August
Rates: $5 per person
Facilities: Cafeteria, shared bathrooms, sports
Notes: Accommodations available to the public on space-available basis only; linens not provided
Telephone: 208-459-5405

The College of Idaho was established in 1891 as a private school affiliated with the Presbyterian Church. The 50-acre campus is located in the town of Caldwell (population 15,000) about 25 miles from Boise, in the southwest corner of the state. Nearby are Lake Lowell, the Snake River, the Rocky Mountains, a game preserve, and a bird sanctuary. The annual Snake River rodeo and stampede are held in the area.

Caldwell, once the site of an Oregon Trail campground, is now best known as a distribution and processing center for agricultural and livestock products and as the seat of an experimental agricultural station. Mobile homes and recreational vehicles are manufactured at Caldwell.

ILLINOIS
The Prairie State
state flower: violet; state bird: cardinal

Illinois is the twenty-first state, admitted to the Union in 1818. The Land of Lincoln is better known for the cities of Chicago and Peoria than for its capital at Springfield. The major components of the state's economy—agriculture, heavy industry, and coal mining—are tied to Illinois's status as a transportation center. The Illinois Waterway, Lake Michigan, and the Mississippi River form a shipping network for the steel, oil, chemicals, meat, machinery, produce, and minerals produced in the state and the entire northern Midwest.

Among the recreational opportunities in the state are boating, swimming, waterskiing, fishing, hunting, ice-skating, ice-boating, ice-fishing, cross-country skiing, tobogganing, and snowmobiling.

College Accommodations

CHICAGO

Situated on Lake Michigan, Chicago has a population of 3 million and is the second-largest city in the United States. It is at the heart of a metropolitan area housing some 7 million people and is the financial, cultural, industrial, and commercial-transportation center of the Midwest. Once called Butcher to the World, the city is now better known for its manufactured products and printing.

Surrounding the Loop in downtown Chicago are the Merchandise Mart, the world's largest commercial building; the Chicago Board of Trade; libraries; the opera and theaters; and many shops. Lakefront attractions include Grant's Park, the Chicago Art Museum, the Field Museum of Natural History, Adler Planetarium, Buckingham Memorial Fountain, and the Shedd Aquarium. The Gold Coast, along the lakeshore, is the site of skyscrapers, hotels, and Lincoln Park, with its 3.5-acre conservatory and zoo.

The South Side has the Museum of Science and Industry, Jackson Park, and the University of Chicago, where the first controlled nuclear reaction took place. In fact, Chicago has 58 colleges and universities and 800 technical schools. Enclaves of every nationality coexist here; the largest are Polish, Chinese, German, Lithuanian, Irish, Greek, and Italian.

DePaul University
Chicago, IL 60604

Rooms available: Third week in June to third week in August
Rates: $50–$60 per week (2-week minimum stay)
Facilities: Cafeteria nearby
Policy on children: Accepted in parents' room
Restrictions: Visitors must have an educationally related purpose
Telephone: 312-321-8020 or 8621

Founded in 1898 by the Vincentian Fathers, DePaul University is a private Catholic institution. Among its facilities are the Frank Lewis Center, in the Loop, and the Lincoln Park campus, in the near north section of the city. The many cultural, social, and recreational offerings of Chicago are available by public transport.

Northern Illinois University
De Kalb, IL 60115

Rooms available: June to August; during the school year, guests are housed at a hotel on campus
Rates: $17 single, $26 double; in hotel, $31.08 single, $36.63 double
Facilities: Cafeteria (available only to large groups), athletic facilities, pool, movies, video games
Policy on children: Accepted
Telephone: 815-753-1586

Northern Illinois University is a state-associated school founded in 1893. The 449-acre campus is in the city of De Kalb, 65 miles west of Chicago, and features a lagoon and a wooded area. Nearby is the Great American Railroad Museum, along with many historic sites.

De Kalb (population 32,000), a farming and manufacturing area in northern Illinois, is fairly rural despite its proximity to Chicago. Its growth was stimulated in the 1870s by Joseph Gidden's invention of the first workable barbed wire, something which is now popular among collectors.

Quincy College
Quincy, Il 62301

Rooms available: All year
Rates: $12 single; $9 per person, double
Facilities: Laundry, store, shared bathrooms
Policy on children: Accepted if supervised
Telephone: 800-637-6686

Located in the town of Quincy, the College is a Roman Catholic school operated by the Franciscans. It has a 28-acre campus and is a short distance from the Mississippi River. The school also owns an 80-acre field station for biological research.

Quincy, with a population of about 42,000, has many old river estates and town houses, including the Governor John Wood Mansion, now headquarters for the Historical Society of Quincy and Adams County.

College Accommodations

Shimer College
Waukegan, IL 60085

Rooms available: June 1 to third week in August (reservations required)
Rates: $30 per room (room holds up to 3 people)
Facilities: Bathrooms, kitchenettes, laundry facilities (no linens or cooking utensils supplied)
Policy on children: Accepted
Telephone: 708-623-8400

Shimer College, founded in 1853, is an independent undergraduate college. Its 85-acre suburban campus is in the city of Waukegan (population 66,000), 40 miles north of Chicago. It takes about 45 minutes to reach either Chicago or Milwaukee, Wisconsin, while Marriott's Great America amusement park and the shores of Lake Michigan are each about 15 minutes away.

Waukegan is a residential and industrial city whose magnificent harbor on Lake Michigan makes it the first port of call for ships plying the St. Lawrence Seaway. It was settled in 1835 as Little Fort, near an old French stockade that was, in turn, built on the site of an Indian village.

INDIANA
The Hoosier State
state flower: peony; state bird: cardinal

Admitted to the Union in 1816, Indiana is one of the most interesting states geographically. The Ice Age left lakes (including Lake Michigan) and moraines in its northern third, a southwestward-sloping plain in its center, and the rugged Cumberland Mountains in the southern third. This southern tier is strikingly scenic, characterized by deep wooded valleys and caves.

The capital, Indianapolis, is the site of one of the most famous auto races in the world, the Indy 500, run every Memorial Day weekend. Outstanding recreational possibilities include lake and river water sports, fishing, hiking, hunting, and camping. Some of the places to visit include the Lincoln Boyhood National Memorial, the Wyandotte Caves, and Holiday World at the town of Santa Claus, a 47-acre theme park with areas devoted to Christmas, the Fourth of July, and Halloween.

College Accommodations

Taylor University
Upland, IN 46989

Rooms available: Third week in May to mid-August (reservations required)
Rates: $20.70, including 3 meals; $19.65, including 2 meals; room-only rates also available
Facilities: Cafeteria, store, shared bathrooms, sports facilities
Policy on children: Accepted
Telephone: 800-882-3456

Taylor University is a nonsectarian Christian institution that occupies a campus of some 240 acres in Upland, about midway between Indianapolis and Fort Wayne. It is in a rural setting, and there is a small lake on campus.

IOWA
The Hawkeye State
state flower: wild rose; state bird: eastern goldfinch

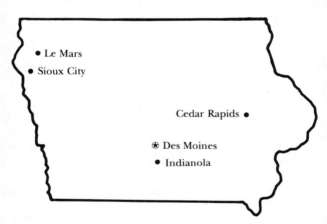

Admitted twenty-ninth to the Union in 1846, the prairie state of Iowa is mostly rich, gently rolling land dissected by many rivers. The exceptions are the hills in the northeast and the bluffs along the Mississippi and Missouri rivers that form the state's eastern and western borders. The capital is Des Moines; other cities of note are Cedar Rapids, Davenport, and Sioux City. Chiefly agricultural, Iowa is a national leader in the production of corn and other grains and the raising of cattle, but food and chemical processing and the manufacturing of machinery are also important to the state economy.

This area of the country was inhabited by Mound Builders in prehistoric times; when white men arrived in the seventeenth century, Iowa, Sac, Fox, and Sioux Indians occupied the land. Mounds built by the earliest inhabitants can be viewed at Effigy Mounds National Monument in the northeastern corner of Iowa.

Other places of interest include the Herbert Hoover National Historic Site and Library, both at West Branch, about 60 miles west of Davenport, and Spillville, where Czech composer Antonin Dvořák spent the summer of 1893 and composed part of his New World Symphony.

Simpson College
Indianola, IA 50125

Rooms available: June and July (reservations required)
Rates: $17 per person and up, depending on type of accommodation
Facilities: Cafeteria, kitchenettes, store, both private and shared bathrooms, multipurpose sports facilities, tennis courts, indoor and outdoor pools
Policy on children: Accepted
Telephone: 515-961-1533

Simpson College, founded in 1860, is historically related to the Methodist Church. Its 55-acre campus is in a suburban area 12 miles from the state capital, Des Moines (population 200,000).

Situated at the junction of the Raccoon and Des Moines rivers, Des Moines is an important industrial and shipping center for the Corn Belt. Many insurance companies are headquartered here. Places of interest include the capitol building; the Des Moines Art Center; the Center of Science and Industry; the State Historical, Memorial and Art Building; the Equitable Building; and 1,700 acres of parks.

Westmar College
Le Mars, IA 51031

Rooms available: June 1 to September
Rates: $5 without linen, $8 with linen

College Accommodations

Westmar College (continued)
Facilities: Cafeteria generally available, gym, computer center
Policy on children: Accepted
Restrictions: No alcohol or pets
Telephone: 712-546-7081

Westmar College, operated by the United Methodist Church, is on an 80-acre campus in a rural area about 25 miles from Sioux City (population 86,000).

Sioux City, in the northwest section of the state, is at the juncture of the Big Sioux, Floyd, and Missouri rivers. It has a huge livestock market, as well as meat-packing, honey, and popcorn-processing plants. In addition to a nearby state park, the city has an art center.

KANSAS
The Sunflower State
state flower: sunflower; state bird: western meadowlark

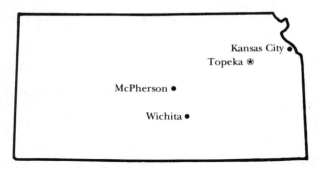

Kansas, the thirty-fourth state, was admitted to the Union in 1861. Its capital is Topeka, while Wichita and Kansas City are the major cities. The state is at the geographic center of the United States; a small monument 2 miles from Lebanon marks the exact spot. Farming, particularly of wheat, is important, although agriculture has been replaced by the manufacture of transportation equipment, chemicals, and aircraft as the state's main sources of income; oil is a potential contributor to the economy.

Kansas played a significant role in the growth of the country. Dodge City and Abilene were jumping-off places for the Wild West, and Fort Leavenworth was one of the first Army posts, although the city of Leavenworth is now better known as the site of a federal prison.

A few of the things to see in Kansas are the Pawnee Indian Village State Historic Site, near Courtland; Boot Hill Museum and Front Street, in Dodge City; the U.S. Cavalry Museum, in Fort Riley; the Dalton Gang Hideout and Museum, in Meade; the Children's Farmstead (a miniature petting and feeding farm), in Overland Park; Old Shawnee Town, in Shawnee; and the Omnisphere and Science Center, in Wichita.

Central College
McPherson, KS 67460

Rooms available: End of May to mid-August
Rates: Call for current rates
Facilities: Laundry, kitchenettes, both private and shared bathrooms, gym, weight room
Policy on children: Accepted
Telephone: 316-241-0723

Central College was founded in 1887 by the Church of the Brethren and is located in a rural area in McPherson, a town of some 13,000 people about 50 miles north of Wichita. McPherson has a museum with many artifacts of the 1920s and the first man-made diamond.

Kansas Newman College
Wichita, KS 67213

Rooms available: June to first week in August
Rates: $10 single
Policy on children: Accepted
Telephone: 316-942-4291

A private liberal arts school affiliated with the Catholic Church, Kansas Newman College is on 55 acres in a suburban area of Wichita (population 285,000), the largest city in Kansas.

Situated at the confluence of the Arkansas and Little Arkansas rivers, Wichita is a commercial and industrial center built on the site of a Wichita Indian village. Among the annual celebrations is the Mid-America All-Indian Center Inter-Tribal Pow Wow, in late July. The city has

Kansas Newman College (continued)

seventy municipal parks for golf, swimming, and other recreation.

KENTUCKY
The Bluegrass State
state flower: goldenrod; state bird: cardinal

The fifteenth state, admitted to the Union in 1792, Kentucky is best known for racehorses and bourbon, although tobacco, coal, machinery, electrical products, chemicals, and metals contribute to its economy. Kentucky lies between the Appalachian Mountains on the east and the Mississippi River on the west; the Ohio River lies to the north.

Among the many places worth a visit in Kentucky are Mammoth Cave National Park and the Lincoln Birthplace Historical Site, near the middle of the state; Cumberland Gap National Historical Park, in the southeast corner; Fort Knox, just south of Louisville; Churchill Downs (where the Kentucky Derby is run on the first Saturday in May) and the Kentucky Derby Museum, both in Louisville; the Bluegrass region, about 1,200 square miles in the north-central part of the state; various distilleries; Appalachian villages; and the Land Between the Lakes National Recreation Area, 170,000 wooded acres in southwestern Kentucky and northwestern Tennessee with more than 200 miles of hiking trails and marked scenic drives. Kentucky's lakes and rivers make for excellent boating, swimming, fishing, skin diving, waterskiing, and rafting; hunting, hiking, and camping are also popular. The major spectator sport, of course, is horse racing.

Transylvania University
Lexington, KY 40508

Rooms available: Accommodations are currently being renovated; call for dates of availability and prices
Telephone: 606-233-8181

Transylvania University, a private coeducational school, was established in 1780, making it the oldest college west of the Allegheny Mountains. Old Morrison, a National Historic Landmark built in 1833, is the administration building on the 27-acre campus.

Lexington (population 210,000) is in the heart of the 1,200-square-mile Bluegrass region in north-central Kentucky. Among the attractions here are Ashland, Henry Clay's home from 1811 to 1852; the Kentucky Horse Park and Man o'War Monument; the Mary Todd Lincoln House; and the Spendthrift Training Center, where Thoroughbreds are trained.

College Accommodations

LOUISIANA
The Pelican State
state flower: magnolia; state bird: eastern brown pelican

Also known as the Bayou State and the Sportsman's Paradise, Louisiana was admitted to the Union as the eighteenth state in 1812. Influenced by British, African, Caribbean, Spanish, and French settlers—especially the French-speaking immigrants from Acadia, or Nova Scotia—Louisiana is an intriguing blend of their cultures. The Cajun (a corruption of Acadian) patois and cuisine and the use of parishes rather than counties as the political subdivision make Louisiana exceptional among the states.

More than 7,000 miles of navigable waterways—rivers, lakes, and bayous—constitute Louisiana's most prominent geographical feature. North of most of these waterways, the land turns into prairie and then low pine-covered hills.

New Orleans' French Quarter is the major tourist attraction, but Acadian Village, 10 miles from Lafayette; Audubon State Commemorative Area, near St. Francisville; and many restored plantations and antebellum mansions are also worth visiting. Fishing, hunting, swimming, camping, and boating are the main forms of outdoor recreation.

NEW ORLEANS

A city of 600,000, most of New Orleans lies between the Mississippi River on the west and south and Lake Pontchartrain on the north. It is situated on a peninsula that separates the Gulf of Mexico from Lake Pontchartrain. As a result, the city has some interesting bridges, including the Greater New Orleans over the Mississippi, one of the longest cantilevers in the country, and the 24-mile-long Lake Pontchartrain Causeway, one of the most spectacular.

The number one tourist attraction in New Orleans is the French Quarter, a seventy-square-block area bordered by Canal Street, Rampart Street, Esplanade Avenue, and the Mississippi River. Within the Quarter are such magnets as Preservation Hall, with its world-famous traditional jazz bands; Jackson Square, the historic center of the city and the site of displays by sidewalk artists; and numerous museums, historic buildings, and excellent restaurants. Just wandering along Bourbon Street—a name to conjure with—is an exciting pastime.

Elsewhere in this picturesque city are many other interesting sights. Among them are Audubon Park and Zoological Garden, Jean Lafitte National Historical Park, Louisiana Nature and Science Center, and a number of nineteenth-century cemeteries. Among the other activities that can be pursued in New Orleans are bayou, swamp, canal, and river cruises; steamboat and paddle-wheel cruises on the Mississippi; cruises to nearby restored plantations; walking tours of the French Quarter and Garden District; rides in horse-drawn surreys; and rides on the St. Charles Avenue streetcar.

Note that all three New Orleans listings are in the University District. They are within walking distance of the streetcar, a National Historic Landmark, and minutes from the French Quarter, the business district, and Audubon Park. Also nearby are the Superdome and many fine restaurants.

College Accommodations

International Center Y
936 St. Charles Avenue
New Orleans, LA 70130

Rooms available: All year
Rates: $20 single; $25 double
Facilities: Restaurant, laundry, shared bathrooms, fitness center, pool
Notes: Reasonably priced all-inclusive tours available
Telephone: 504-568-9622

Loyola University
New Orleans, LA 70118

Rooms available: June to August (reservations required)
Rates: $30 single; $25 per person, double
Facilities: Cafeteria, laundry, kitchenettes, both private and shared bathrooms, recreational complex
Policy on children: Accepted
Telephone: 504-865-2445

Loyola University was founded in 1912. A private school operated by the Sisters of Jesus, it occupies seven blocks in a residential area of New Orleans.

Tulane University
New Orleans, LA 70118

Rooms available: June and July (reservations preferred)
Rates: $25 single, $32 double with linen; $22.50 single, $28 double without linen
Facilities: Cafeteria, laundry, kitchenettes, both private and shared bathrooms, recreation center with pools and courts, summer theater
Policy on children: Accepted
Telephone: 504-865-5426

Tulane University, established in 1834, is a private, nonsectarian institution. The campus faces St. Charles Avenue and is adjacent to Loyola University. The main campus consists of 100 acres in the Garden District of New Orleans.

MAINE
The Pine Tree State
state flower: white-pine cone and tassel; state bird: chickadee

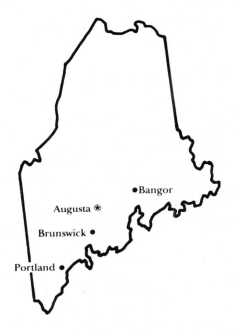

Maine, the largest of the New England states, was the twenty-third to be admitted to the Union, in 1820. Its Atlantic shoreline is quite rugged for most of its length, but from Kennebec to the New Hampshire border there are some sandy beaches. This area, along with that around Bar Harbor, attracts most summertime visitors.

Maine's economy is based on forest products (shipbuilding, lumber, pulp and paper), textiles, granite, leather goods, potatoes, and lobster. Blessed with many rivers and lakes, to say nothing of the Atlantic Ocean, Maine is a mecca for lovers of water sports. From windjammer cruises to canoeing, there's something for everyone here. Fishing, camping, and horse racing are also popular. In winter, skiing, ice-skating, sledding, and snowmobiling are available throughout the state.

College Accommodations

Bowdoin College
Brunswick, ME 04011

Rooms available: June through mid-August
Rates: $25 single; $35 double; $5 children
Facilities: Cafeteria, sports
Policy on children: Accepted
Notes: Attractions include concerts, arts festival, summer theater, Peary-McMillan Arctic Museum
Telephone: 207-725-3100

Bowdoin College, founded in 1794, is Maine's oldest institution of higher learning. A private school, its 110-acre campus is located in a rural area in the town of Brunswick (population 18,000), which is near the coast and 26 miles from Portland. Bowdoin was the college of Hawthorne and Longfellow, and it houses the famed Hawthorne-Longfellow Library; Harriet Beecher Stowe wrote *Uncle Tom's Cabin* in 1851 while serving on the Bowdoin faculty.

Brunswick, on the Androscoggin River and Casco Bay, was settled in 1628 and incorporated in 1738. A central location for touring midcoast Maine, Brunswick is close to Boothbay Harbor, Kennebunkport, and the Bath Marine Museum.

MARYLAND
The Old Line State
state flower: black-eyed Susan; state bird: Baltimore oriole

One of the original thirteen colonies and the site of the federal capital, Maryland is rich in history. Among the important places to visit are Fort McHenry, where the U.S. flag flew during the War of 1812, inspiring the poem by Francis Scott Key that became the words of the national anthem; Annapolis, the state capital and home of the U.S. Naval Academy; Antietam National Battlefield, where the bloodiest battle of the Civil War took place on September 17, 1862; and, of course, the District of Columbia.

Baltimore, whose waterfront and downtown areas have been undergoing a restoration in recent years, contains such attractions as the Baltimore & Ohio Railroad Museum; Babe Ruth's Birthplace Museum and the Maryland Baseball Hall of Fame; the National Aquarium; and the U.S. frigate *Constellation,* the country's oldest warship, launched in 1797.

Recreation is centered on the Atlantic shore and the Allegheny Mountains, while the many miles of seashore bordering Chesapeake Bay—which sharply divides the state—are fertile grounds for water sports, fishing, bird-watching, clam-digging, and beachcombing. The unusual official state sport is a modern version of jousting.

College of Notre Dame of Maryland
Baltimore, MD 21210

Rooms available: June 1 to August 15 (accommodations limited; reservations required)
Rates: $20
Facilities: Swimming pool, tennis courts
Policy on children: Accepted
Restrictions: No pets
Notes: Campus is on bus line to downtown Baltimore
Telephone: 301-532-5381

The College of Notre Dame, founded in 1873, is a private liberal arts school for women. The 55-acre campus, which is in a suburban area of Baltimore, offers exceptional resources for history buffs and art lovers.

Baltimore, a city of nearly 1 million, was incorporated in 1745. Situated on the Patapsco River estuary, an arm of Chesapeake Bay, it is a seaport and a commercial and industrial center.

College Accommodations

Washington Bible College
Lanham, MD 20706

Rooms available: Late May to mid-August (reservations required)
Rates: $15 per person (no linens provided)
Facilities: Cafeteria, laundry, shared bathrooms, swimming pool, tennis, sports facilities
Policy on children: Accepted
Restrictions: No pets, no smoking or drinking on campus
Telephone: 301-552-1400

Washington Bible College is a private school in a suburban area 12 miles from downtown Washington, D.C., and 22 miles from Baltimore.

Columbia Union College
Takoma Park, MD 20912

Rooms available: All year, as available
Rates: $22.50–$25 in dorms; $40 in motel rooms with 2 double beds
Facilities: Cafeteria, snack bar, shared baths in dorms, private baths in motel rooms
Policy on children: Accepted
Notes: Since this is a Seventh-Day Adventist school, all meals are vegetarian, coffee is decaf, etc.
Telephone: 301-891-4178 for dorm accommodations, 301-891-4161 for motel rooms

Located on a 2-acre urban campus, Columbia Union College is just 10 miles from Washington, D.C. It was established by the Seventh-Day Adventist Church in 1904 and offers the advantages of a small town with a big city just a short ride away by bus and subway.

MASSACHUSETTS
The Bay State
state flower: mayflower; state bird: chickadee

One of the original thirteen colonies, Massachusetts abounds in truly historic spots: Plymouth, where the *Mayflower* landed in 1620; Salem, infamous for the witch trials of the 1690s; Boston, site of the "tea party" that was a factor in the start of the American Revolution; Concord, where "the shot heard round the world" was fired on April 19, 1775, the morning after Paul Revere's midnight ride.

In addition, the state is home to such attractions as the 28,000-acre Cape Cod National Seashore, Martha's Vineyard, Massachusetts Institute of Technology, Harvard University, the 1623 town of Gloucester on Cape Ann, and Minute Man National Historical Park, to name but a few. Enthusiasts of American literature can visit Walden Pond, remembered for its association with Henry David Thoreau, and the study in which Ralph Waldo Emerson worked. For recreation, there are all manner of water sports on the Atlantic coast and hiking and camping in the Berkshire Hills along the state's western border.

University of Massachusetts at Amherst
Amherst, MA 01003

Rooms available: June to third week in August (reservations required)
Rates: $18 single; $25 double

College Accommodations

University of Massachusetts at Amherst (continued)
Facilities: Restaurant, snack bars, coffee shops, athletic facilities, fine arts center
Policy on children: Accepted
Telephone: 413-545-2591

The Amherst campus of the University of Massachusetts occupies the original site of the school, established in 1863. The 1,100-acre campus is in the city of Amherst (population 15,000), which is in the Connecticut Valley, a picturesque area about 90 miles west of Boston.

A lovely college town with tree-lined streets, Amherst was the birthplace and residence of Emily Dickinson. Nearby are Tanglewood, where a world-famous music festival is held every year; historic Deerfield; Old Sturbridge Village, a re-created New England town of the 1830s; Quabbin Reservoir; and several golf courses.

BOSTON

Boston (population 571,000) is the state capital and the largest city in Massachusetts. A fascinating study in past and present, the broad avenues of today's metropolis vanish into the crooked streets of Colonial Boston; modern stores stand next to old churches and shrines of the American Revolution.

Tales of the nation's early days come to life with visits to museums and historic landmarks: Boston Common, the country's oldest public park; Old North Church, from whose steeple Paul Revere signaled that British soldiers were coming; Faneuil Hall, where meetings of those influential in the Revolutionary movement were held; Granary Burying Ground, where John Hancock, Samuel Adams, Paul Revere, Peter Faneuil, and the parents of Benjamin Franklin are buried. Every visitor should walk the 3-mile Freedom Trail, which begins at the visitor center of Boston National Historical Park at 25 State Street and takes participants on a circuit of sites important in the nation's early history.

Among other activities in Boston are boat tours of Boston Harbor and cruises along the Charles River; walking tours of the Black Heritage Trail and the harbor; and shopping in the elegant stores of

Copley Place, in the eclectic Quincy Market, or at Downtown Crossing, a pedestrian mall and Boston's original shopping area.

Boston Central Y
316 Huntington Avenue
Boston, MA 02115

Rooms available: All year
Rates: $27 single; $40 double, including breakfast
Facilities: Cafeteria, swimming pool, fitness center
Telephone: 617-536-7800

Garden Halls Dormitories
164 Marlborough Street
Boston, MA 02116

Rooms available: Third week in June to third week in August
Rates: $22 per person (3-day stay, no linens provided)
Policy on children: Accepted
Restrictions: No cooking in rooms; parking not available
Telephone: 617-267-0079

The Garden Halls Dormitories were set up in Boston's Back Bay to provide housing for the many students in the area who could find no rooms at their own institution.

North East Residence Hall
204 Bay State Road
Boston, MA 02215

Rooms available: June 1 to September 1
Rates: $25 single; $20 per person, double
Facilities: Laundry, shared bathrooms
Telephone: 617-247-8318

Located near Boston University, a stay in this residence hall offers the traveler an opportunity to see Boston, with its many historic and cultural sites.

Fitchburg State College
Fitchburg, MA 01420-2697

Rooms available: June 1 to mid-August (reservations required)
Rates: $24 single; $12 per person, double
Facilities: Cafeteria, laundry, kitchenettes, store, some private bathrooms, extensive sports facilities, tennis
Policy on children: Accepted
Notes: Trains to Boston are available
Telephone: 617-345-2151

Located on a 90-acre site, Fitchburg State College was founded in 1894 as a state-supported school. It is located in an urban area, about 45 miles from Boston and 75 miles from Worcester.

In addition to a wealth of historic and cultural opportunities in the area, Fitchburg (population 40,000) offers camping, fishing, swimming, and antique shops galore. Fitchburg is also noted for its art museum. Concord, about 40 miles away, is the site of the Battle of Concord; the First Continental Congress, presided over by John Hancock in 1774; and the homes of Thoreau, Emerson, Hawthorne, and the Alcotts.

Bentley College
Waltham, MA 02154

Rooms available: June to mid-August (reservations and deposit required)
Rates: $50 for 1-bedroom suite including 2 beds, private bath, kitchenette, living room; $75 for 2 bedrooms (linens and continental breakfast on weekday mornings provided; 3-night minimum stay)
Facilities: Cafeteria, laundry, kitchenettes, private bathrooms, campus store, tennis courts, pool, free parking
Policy on children: Accepted
Telephone: 617-891-2273 in state, 800-292-8787 outside

Founded in 1817 as a private college, Bentley is located in a suburban area about 9 miles from Boston. It occupies 110 acres of hilltop tranquility. Nearby are the beaches of Cape Cod, the outlet stores at Kittery, Maine, and of course, historic Boston.

MICHIGAN
The Great Lake State
state flower: apple blossom; state bird: robin

Michigan was admitted to the Union as the twenty-sixth state in 1837. Its capital is Lansing, but the larger cities of Detroit, Flint, and Grand Rapids are better known. Although it gained its early reputation as the automobile capital of the nation, it is also known as the home of the "Motown Sound." Agriculture and fishing contribute heavily to the economy, and tourism, especially along the Great Lakes beaches, is growing in importance.

Michigan fronts on four of the five Great Lakes and consists of two very different sections, the Upper and Lower peninsulas. It has over 1,100 lakes and more miles of lakeshore than any other state. Mackinac Island, which bans cars, is a favorite vacation resort. Michigan has ski areas and parks galore. In addition, the Henry Ford Museum and Greenfield Village just outside Detroit are of great interest.

DETROIT

Michigan's largest city (population 1,500,000) and the fifth-largest city in the United States, Detroit is actually north of Windsor, Canada, to which it is connected by the Ambassador Bridge. The city is located on the Detroit River between Lakes Erie and St. Clair and is a major U.S. port of entry and a shipping and rail center. Initially renowned for the carriages built there, Detroit became the automotive capital of the world as a result of Henry Ford's pioneering use of the assembly line.

Not for those who prefer to loll around, Detroit is an active city whose sights include the Detroit Institute of Arts; a historical museum; Cobo Hall, one of the world's largest exhibition halls; and the Renaissance Center, a new group of buildings combining a degree of high-rise beauty with the better aspects of a single-story shopping mall. Belle Isle, in the Detroit River, is a public park with gardens, walking areas, a conservatory, an aquarium, and a children's zoo.

Mercy College of Detroit
Detroit, MI 48219

Rooms available: All year, except certain holidays
Rates: $22 per person for a guest room
Facilities: Cafeteria, adjoining bathrooms
Policy on children: Accepted
Telephone: 313-592-6170

Mercy College was founded in 1941 and is a coeducational college located in urban northwestern Detroit. Nearby are Greenfield Village, the Henry Ford Museum, the Detroit Institute of Arts, the Greek Inn, and Balboa Amusement Park. Windsor, Canada, is a short drive away.

Calvin College
Grand Rapids, MI 49506

Rooms available: Selected dates between mid-May and mid-August

Rates: $12 per person; $6 for children aged 5–16, free for children under 5
Facilities: Kitchenettes, shared bathrooms, store, gym, pool
Telephone: 616-957-6280

Organized in 1876, Calvin College is affiliated with the Christian Reformed Church and occupies a 166-acre suburban site about 6 miles from downtown Grand Rapids.

Although it is much smaller than Detroit, with a population of 185,000, Grand Rapids is Michigan's second most populous city. It still leads in the production of the high-grade furniture for which it first gained renown. Of note are the city's Grand Center and Vandenburg Center, with its Calder sculpture. The Gerald R. Ford Museum is a very modern structure, and the Grand Rapids Public Museum offers exhibits on the history of furniture.

Northwood Institute
Midland, MI 48640

Rooms available: June, July, and August (reservations required)
Rates: Starting at around $8 per person, depending on type of accommodation
Facilities: Cafeteria, laundry, kitchenettes, private bathrooms, store, pool, tennis, jogging paths
Policy on children: Accepted
Telephone: 517-832-4375

Founded in 1959 as an independent college, Northwood has a 280-acre campus located in a suburban area 70 miles from Saginaw and 125 miles from Detroit

Midland (population 37,000) is in the Saginaw Valley at the confluence of the Tittabawassee and Chippewa rivers. The city owes its development to the Dow Chemical Company, whose corporate headquarters are there. Large deposits of salt attracted the company to Midland and are the basis for many products. Dow Gardens, the Automotive Hall of Fame, and Midland Center for the Arts contribute to the cultural life in Midland.

Saginaw Valley State University
University Center, MI 48710

Rooms available: Mid-May to mid-August (reservations required)
Rates: $10 single; $6.25 per person, double
Facilities: Limited, with only a laundry available and shared bathrooms; for families, a suite with private bath is occasionally available
Policy on children: Accepted
Telephone: 517-790-4255

The University was founded in 1963 and occupies a campus of 780 acres 5 miles from Saginaw.

Saginaw has about 75,000 residents and was originally a lumbering center. It now grows such items as beans and sugar beets and is probably best known as an automotive center. The city has many attractive parks, as well as the Historical Society Museum and the Art Museum.

Eastern Michigan University
Ypsilanti, MI 48197

Rooms available: Summer months, as available
Rates: $18–$30, depending on type of accommodation (single rooms and suites available)
Policy on children: Accepted
Notes: Conference center is heavily booked for meetings; campus attractions include films, orchestral concerts, jazz ensembles, theatrical productions
Telephone: 313-487-1157, 800-351-4058

Eastern Michigan University was founded in 1849 as a state-supported school. The 460-acre campus is located in Ypsilanti, population 30,000. This is a suburban area 6 miles east of Ann Arbor and 35 miles west of Detroit.

Ypsilanti is a residential, commercial, and farming center. Attractions in the vicinity include Ypsilanti Historical Museum, Depot Town, and tours of General Motors.

MINNESOTA
The North Star State
state flower: showy lady slipper; state bird: common loon

Minnesota is the thirty-second state, admitted to the Union in 1858. The capital, St. Paul, is considerably smaller than its twin city of Minneapolis. While agriculture, especially soybeans and dairy products, is important, manufacturing employs a greater proportion of the population. The Mesabi Range, at one time the greatest iron-ore producer in America, still yields ore in the form of iron pellets.

The state makes full use of its 10,000 lakes for fishing, and its rivers are interesting in that some run north to Hudson Bay while others, such as the Mississippi, run south. National parks, the Minnesota Symphony Orchestra, and the Shakespeare Festival are among the state's attractions. The Mayo Clinic, in Rochester, draws patients from around the world.

Bemidji State University
Bemidji, MN 56601

Rooms available: All year
Rates: $9.50 single; $15 per double room
Facilities: Cafeteria, laundry, shared bathrooms
Policy on children: Accepted
Restrictions: Alcohol forbidden on University premises
Telephone: 218-755-3750

Bemidji State was founded in 1919. The 89-acre campus is located in a rural area on the shores of Lake Bemidji, about 230 miles north of Minneapolis.

Bemidji is a summer and winter resort and sportfishing area, with its major industry being tourism, and year-round recreational facilities abound for swimming, boating, downhill and cross-country skiing, and snowmobiling. The lakefront features an 18-foot figure of Paul Bunyan and his ox.

Saint John's University
Collegeville, MN 56321

Rooms available: June to mid-August
Rates: $18 single; $12 per person, double
Facilities: Cafeteria
Policy on children: Accepted
Restrictions: Rules regarding alcohol and the use of the grounds are available on registration
Telephone: 612-363-3487

Established in 1857, Saint John's University is a Catholic institution occupying some 2,400 acres of woodland and lakes in a rural area west of Minneapolis. It is the site of St. John's Abbey and Church.

The large number of lakes on campus means good fishing, and there is a golf course nearby. For those wishing the peace and quiet of a rural setting, this is the place.

College of St. Scholastica
Duluth, MN 55811

Rooms available: First week of June to third week of August (reservations required)

Rates: Variable, according to type of accommodation (from dorm to apartment)
Facilities: Cafeteria, laundry, both private and shared bathrooms, store, tennis, basketball
Policy on children: Accepted
Telephone: 218-723-6396

The College, founded in 1912, is affiliated with the Catholic Church. It has a 160-acre campus in a suburban area about 10 minutes from Duluth. There are numerous trails and wooded areas on campus. Lake Superior and its recreational resources are nearby.

Duluth, a city of 100,000, was incorporated in 1870 and is at the western end of Lake Superior, one of the largest lakes in the world. The city is the commercial, industrial, and cultural center for northern Minnesota and was named after an early explorer who found Indian settlements here in 1670.

Mankato State University
Mankato, MN 56001

Rooms available: First week in June to third week in August
Rates: $15 single; $10 per person, double
Facilities: Cafeteria, kitchenettes, laundry, shared bathrooms, store, swimming, tennis, volleyball, weight room, summer theater
Policy on children: Accepted, under parental supervision
Restrictions: No alcohol, no smoking except in designated areas
Telephone: 507-389-1011

Mankato is a state school located on 165 acres in a rural area 70 miles south of Minneapolis.

The town of Mankato (population 31,000) is at the juncture of the Minnesota and Blue Earth rivers. Mankato is an Indian word for blue earth, the clay that lines the riverbanks. The Blue Earth County Historical Society Museum is the site of an 1871 mansion, a restored log cabin, and other pioneer displays. Minneopa State Park has two large waterfalls and a wind-driven gristmill. Mankato is a trade and processing center for a farming and dairy region, and Mankato stone has been quarried there for over 200 years. There are also woolen mills, grain mills, and a brewery in the area.

College Accommodations

Southwest State University
Marshall, MN 56258

Rooms available: Summer
Rates: $10 per person (2-week maximum stay)
Facilities: Cafeteria
Policy on children: Not accepted
Telephone: 507-537-6286

Located some 150 miles from Minneapolis, Southwest State was founded in 1960 and occupies a rural site of 200 acres. Campus attractions include a museum, a planetarium, and a theater. Nearby are state parks, lakes, and Pipestone National Monument.

Both Minneapolis and the state as a whole have been greatly underrated by potential visitors. Although farming is very important, Minnesota has more than its share of lakes, rivers, and forests, so hiking, fishing, and hunting are common forms of recreation.

College of St. Catherine
St. Paul, MN 55105

Rooms available: June 1 to August 1
Rates: $14 single; $20 double; $25 triple
Facilities: Cafeteria, laundry, kitchenettes, both private and shared bathrooms, store, pool, tennis courts
Policy on children: Accepted
Telephone: 612-690-6512

The College of St. Catherine, founded in 1905, is a Catholic liberal arts institution, operated by the Sisters of St. Joseph of Carondolet. Its 110-acre campus is located in an urban area midway between Minneapolis and St. Paul.

St. Paul is a city of about 350,000, incorporated in 1854. It is situated on a bluff along the Mississippi and is the twin city of Minneapolis. St. Paul is the capital of Minnesota and is an industrial, commercial, and cultural center for a vast region. It originated as the fur-trading center of Fort Snelling, and in 1841 Father Gautier established St. Paul's Church there, from which the city took its name. For many years considered secondary to Minneapolis, St. Paul is now thought to be the more livable city. The capitol, built in 1904, was modeled after St. Peter's in Rome and has the largest unsupported marble dome in the country. Also of interest are the high-rise city hall made of woods from around the world and the Science Museum of Minnesota.

University of Minnesota Technical College, Waseca
Waseca, MN 56093

Rooms available: April to mid-September (reservations required)
Rates: $8 per person
Facilities: Cafeteria, laundry, kitchenettes, private bathrooms, tennis, exercise center
Policy on children: Accepted
Telephone: 507-835-1000

The University of Minnesota was founded in 1851 and has several campuses. The Waseca campus is located near Clear Lake in the southwest corner of the state. In a state of 10,000 lakes, several of them on campus, the area offers excellent opportunities for water sports.

MISSISSIPPI
The Magnolia State
state flower: magnolia; state bird: mockingbird

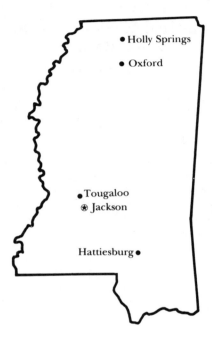

The twentieth state, Mississippi was admitted to the Union in 1817. Its capital and largest city is Jackson; other cities of note include Biloxi, Hattiesburg, and Natchez. With the exception of the flat plain between the Mississippi and Yazoo rivers known as the Mississippi Delta, the state is generally hilly. Cotton is the principal crop in the Delta, while gas and oil production and fishing are of major importance.

Mississippi, with its historic battlefields, antebellum mansions, and comparatively long history as a settled area, is an interesting place to visit.

Mississippi

Rust College
Holly Springs, MS 38635

Rooms available: End of May to mid-August (reservations required)
Rates: $5 per person; linens $2
Facilities: Cafeteria, shared bathrooms
Policy on children: Accepted
Notes: Although the College is available primarily for groups such as family reunions and church retreats, some individuals can be accepted
Telephone: 601-252-4661

Rust College, established in 1866 as a private college under the auspices of the Methodist Church, occupies 120 acres in a small town 35 miles from Memphis.

Holly Springs has about 8,000 residents. It was subjected to about eighty raids during the Revolutionary War, and about 100 residences built before that time survive. Holly Springs is the birthplace of Kate Freeman Clark, an artist who signed her works Freeman Clark to conceal her identity as a woman. Some 1,000 of her paintings are on exhibition in the Kate Freeman Clark Gallery.

Tougaloo College
Tougaloo, MS 39174

Rooms available: During July
Rates: Variable, depending on number in group (groups preferred)
Facilities: Cafeteria
Restrictions: There are strict rules regarding alcohol, drugs, gambling, curfew, etc.
Telephone: 601-956-4941

Tougaloo College, established in 1869, is a liberal arts college affiliated with the United Christian Missionary Society. The 500-acre campus is in a suburban area near Jackson and the Ross Barnett Reservoir. It is primarily a black college.

Jackson, situated on the Pearl River, is the state capital of Mississippi and has many buildings of historic interest. The Governor's Mansion and Old Capitol, built in 1839, is preserved as a museum. The City Hall was used as a hospital during the Civil War. Also of interest are Mynelle Gar-

Tougaloo College (continued)

dens, a state wildlife museum and park, a planetarium, the Mississippi Museum of Arts, and many antebellum houses.

MISSOURI
The Show Me State
state flower: hawthorn; state bird: bluebird

Missouri, the twenty-fourth state, was admitted to the Union in 1821. Its capital is Jefferson City; other major metropolitan centers are Kansas City, St. Louis, and Springfield. Independence, Missouri, is perhaps best known as the birthplace of President Harry S. Truman, although it is a very historic center, having been the beginning of the Santa Fe, Oregon, and California trails. In addition to housing the Truman Library, Independence is also the location of several old buildings and museums, as well as several important Mormon sites.

The state is important for agriculture and manufacturing. The Mississippi River and the Ozark Mountains form part of the state and help to give it a Southern feeling.

Lincoln University
Jefferson City, MO 65101

Rooms available: May, June, and July (reservations required 7 days in advance)
Rates: $12
Facilities: Cafeteria, shared bathrooms, day-care center
Policy on children: Accepted
Telephone: 314-681-5104

Lincoln University was established in 1866 and is a state-controlled school. It occupies 52 acres in Jefferson City and also has two farms of some 522 acres for agricultural instruction. The University is located about 27 miles from the Lake of the Ozarks, and the state capitol building is on campus.

Missouri Southern State College
Joplin, MO 64801

Rooms available: June 1 to August 1 (to groups of at least 10)
Rates: $8 per person (3-day minimum stay)
Facilities: Cafeteria, shared bathrooms, snack bar, pool, video machines
Policy on children: Accepted
Restrictions: No alcohol on campus
Telephone: 417-625-9300

The College, established in 1937, has a 350-acre campus in suburban Joplin.

Joplin, a city of 39,000, was incorporated in 1873 at the edge of the Ozarks in southwest Missouri. It is a railroad center, the shipping and processing point of a grain and livestock region, and has dairy and fruit farms. At one time it was a mining center. Of interest in the city are the Tri-State Mineral Museum, Dorothea Hoover Historical Museum, and Spira Art Center.

KANSAS CITY

Perhaps surprisingly for a prairie city, Kansas City has tree-lined boulevards and many statues and sky-

Kansas City (continued)

scrapers. Site of the Board of Trade, millions of bushels of grain are traded daily using the "public outcry" system. Visitors are welcome to see this activity. The city has its share of shops and shopping centers and makes full use of the limestone caverns that underlie it to store foreign goods amid a 6-mile network of roads and rail lines.

Since Kansas City is located on the Missouri River, sightseeing by boat is popular, as are walking tours. There are museums and art galleries, several parks, and an amusement park for the diversion of visitors.

Rockhurst College
Kansas City, MO 64110

Rooms available: June to mid-August
Rates: Call for current rates
Facilities: Cafeteria available only when there are large groups on campus
Policy on children: Accepted
Telephone: 816-926-4125

Rockhurst College was established in 1910 and is affiliated with the Roman Catholic Church. Its 25-acre campus is located in a residential area of Kansas City. The campus is close to the Plaza, Nelson Art Gallery, and Linda Hall Library.

Park College
Parkville, MO 64152

Rooms available: All year, on a limited basis
Rates: $10 per person, winter; $15 per person, summer (no linens at any time)
Facilities: Cafeteria, pool, track, tennis courts
Policy on children: Accepted
Telephone: 816-741-2000

Park College, founded in 1875, is affiliated with the Reorganized Church of Latter-day Saints. The 800-acre campus is in a suburban area 10 miles from the adjoining cities of Kansas City, Kansas, and Kansas City, Missouri, which are located at the junction of the Missouri and Kansas rivers. They form a large commercial, industrial, and cultural center.

Kansas City, Kansas, is home to the Agricultural Hall of Fame, the Shawnee Mission of 1839, and the Civic Center Mall incorporating a nineteenth-century Indian cemetery. Kansas City, Missouri, is the site of fine parks, amusement areas, the Kansas City Museum of History and Science, and the Miniature Museum.

Lindenwood College
St. Charles, MO 63301

Rooms available: May through August (reservations required)
Rates: $16–$26, depending on the type of accommodation
Facilities: Cafeteria, kitchenettes, both private and shared bathrooms, outdoor pool, gymnasium
Policy on children: Accepted
Telephone: 314-949-2000

Lindenwood College, founded in 1827, is situated on 140 beautifully wooded acres 20 miles from St. Louis.

St. Charles (population 37,000) is nestled on the shores of the Missouri River. Daniel Boone and his family settled in the area in the 1790s, while German immigrants flooded the area from 1832 to 1870 and developed the town into a shopping area for the surrounding farms. Walking tours of an eight-block historic area are conducted by guides in costume, and mid-August features a fair, crafts, and food in a nineteenth-century atmosphere. The St. Louis Zoo, Six Flags over Mid-America, municipal opera in Fred Park, and the various Mississippi River attractions appeal to visitors.

Washington University
St. Louis, MO 63130

Rooms available: June to mid-August
Rates: $14 single; $12 per person, double
Facilities: Cafeteria, laundry, store, shared bathrooms, swimming, tennis, gym, art gallery

College Accommodations

Washington University (continued)
Policy on children: Accepted
Telephone: 314-889-5073

Washington University is a private school established in 1853. The 176-acre campus is located in St. Louis across from Forest Park, which contains a zoo, an opera house, a science center, golfing, and bicycle paths.

St. Louis has five universities and twenty-six colleges and offers a diversity unknown in many other parts of the country. Home of both Busch Stadium and the Gateway Arch, the city also has a wide selection of museums and galleries, old structures and modern ones. A visitors' center is located at the 630-foot-high arch and offers movies and a tram ride to the top.

MONTANA
The Treasure State
state flower: bitterroot; state bird: western meadowlark

Admitted to the Union as the forty-first state in 1889, Montana is sparsely populated and still relatively undeveloped. Its capital is Helena; the largest cities are Billings, Great Falls, Butte, and Missoula. The terrain ranges from broad plains in the east to the Rocky Mountains in the west. Copper, gold, zinc, coal, and petroleum are of great importance, while hydroelectric power is increasingly a factor in the economy.

The state's wilderness areas, along with Glacier National Park and part of Yellowstone National Park, are becoming more and more attractive to tourists. Visitors revel in the swimming, fishing, and hunting as well as the spectacular scenery for which Montana is famous.

Eastern Montana College
Billings, MT 59101-0298

Rooms available: All year
Rates: $10 single; $8 per person, double
Facilities: Cafeteria, grill and deli, swimming pool, tennis, indoor running track, racquetball
Policy on children: Accepted
Restrictions: No pets, alcohol permitted in rooms only
Telephone: 406-657-2333 or 2218

Eastern Montana is a state-supported school that was founded in 1927 and is located in Montana's largest city, Billings. Cooke City and Yellowstone River Rimrocks overlook the campus.

Billings is a city of about 70,000 located on the Yellowstone River and surrounded by mountains. It is a trade and manufacturing center. The Union Pacific Railroad first settled the city, laying it out and naming it after Frederick Billings, president of the railroad.

Montana College of Mineral Science and Technology
Butte, MT 50701

Rooms available: All year
Rates: $10 per person
Facilities: Laundry, private bathrooms, game room, TV room, sport center, swimming pool, racquetball
Policy on children: Accepted
Telephone: 800-445-8324

Located in Butte, one of Montana's larger cities with a population of about 35,000, the school has its own Mineral Museum. Butte is home to a very large open-pit mine, the Art Chateau built in 1898 in the style of a French chateau, and the Copper King Mansion, a fully restored and furnished Victorian mansion built in 1884 by W. A. Clark, one of Montana's leading mine owners. Butte also has a high-

Montana College of Mineral Science and Technology (continued)

altitude sports center that includes roller- and speed-skating rinks and is free to members of the public, except during special events.

NEBRASKA
The Cornhusker State
state flower: goldenrod; state bird: western meadowlark

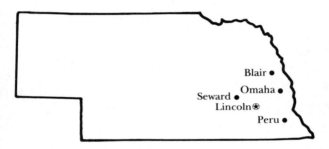

Nebraska was admitted to the Union as the thirty-seventh state in 1867. Its capital is Lincoln, while the largest city is Omaha. Omaha is famous as a packing center for the agricultural produce of the state; Lincoln is known as the headquarters for several major insurance companies.

Arbor Day, which has been set aside for the planting of trees, originated in Nebraska. Willa Cather, still a widely read novelist, was a native. Father Flanagan's Boys Town is located near Omaha. Nebraska's many fresh and alkaline lakes lure fishermen.

Dana College
Blair, NE 68008

Rooms available: June, July, and August
Rates: $16 single; $24 double
Facilities: Cafeteria, bathroom for every 2 rooms, swimming pool
Policy on children: Accepted

Restrictions: No alcohol permitted
Telephone: 402-426-4101

Dana College was founded in 1884 as Trinity College by Danish immigrants. In 1894 it merged with Elk Horn College and took its present name. The 250-acre campus is located in a rural setting on rolling hills about 14 miles from Omaha. On campus are Danish artifacts, the Lauritz Melchior Memorial, and the Queen's Rose Garden.

Nearby in Omaha are Boys Town, the Union Pacific Museum, the Joslyn Museum, and the DeSoto Wildlife Refuge.

Omaha Y
430 South 20th Street
Omaha, NE 68102

Rooms available: All year
Rates: $18 single (private bath extra); $24.50 double (including private bath)
Facilities: Cafeteria, swimming pool, fitness center
Telephone: 402-341-1600

Omaha is home to several large insurance companies and to the Strategic Air Command. Mutual of Omaha has a "wild kingdom" exhibit, while the Strategic Air Command has its own museum. Other points of interest include the Civic Auditorium, the restored Bank of Florence (first built in 1856), and the Great Plains Black Museum. The Old Market area, with its art galleries, boutiques, restaurants, and theaters, has a special attraction to those looking for a taste of the past.

Peru State College
Peru, NE 68421

Rooms available: June 1 to August 15 (reservations required)
Rates: $8 per person
Facilities: Cafeteria, campus store, shared bathrooms
Policy on children: Accepted
Telephone: 800-948-8177

Peru State College was established in 1867, the same year Nebraska became a state. It is located in Peru, some 60

Peru State College (continued)

miles south of Omaha, and is known as the "campus of a thousand oaks." It overlooks the Missouri River, with ready access to Brownville and the *Belle of Brownville,* a riverboat. The campus has a state arboretum and a sports center available to the public.

Concordia Teachers College
Seward, NE 68434

Rooms available: Second week in June through third week in August
Rates: $8 per person
Facilities: Cafeteria open weekdays, bowling, tennis
Notes: Rooms are primarily for educational purposes and conferences; campus has a number of interesting sculptures
Telephone: 402-643-3651

Concordia is affiliated with the Missouri Synod of the Lutheran Church. The 120-acre campus is located in a rural environment 25 miles from the state capital of Lincoln. Nearby are lakes for fishing and water sports.

Lincoln, a city of 171,000, is the trade, industrial, and railroad center for a large grain and livestock region. The city was founded in 1864 as Lancaster and was renamed when it was chosen as the state capital in 1867. The state capitol building is an outstanding example of modern architecture and is richly ornamented. Fairview, the home of William Jennings Bryan, and Thomas Kennard House are historic restorations.

NEW HAMPSHIRE
The Granite State
state flower: lilac; state bird: purple finch

New Hampshire was one of the original thirteen colonies, and its capital is historic Concord; Manchester and Nashua are the largest cities.

Although it is a rocky state, with a mountain view from almost every quarter, New Hampshire is highly industrialized. Major products are leather and leather goods, textiles, lumber, paper goods, and machinery. However, the main industry is tourism, with hiking, fishing, ocean beaches, and swimming in Lake Winnipesaukee popular in the summer and mountain ski resorts equally popular in the winter.

Franklin Pierce College
Rindge, NH 03461

Rooms available: Memorial Day to Labor Day
Rates: From about $12 to $15 per person
Facilities: Cafeteria, coffeehouse, shared bathrooms, boating, tennis, theater, films, golf, hiking
Telephone: 603-899-5111

A private college, Franklin Pierce was founded in 1962 and occupies some 750 acres in a rural town about 65 miles from Boston in southwest New Hampshire.

Rindge is primarily a summer resort overlooking the Monadnock Valley. The valley has a number of lakes and ponds for fishing, swimming, and boating. Of interest is the Cathedral of the Pines, a nondenominational memorial to Americans, particularly women, who died in various wars. It was built of stones from each state and is open for meditation from May to October each year.

NEW JERSEY
The Garden State
state flower: purple violet; state bird: eastern goldfinch

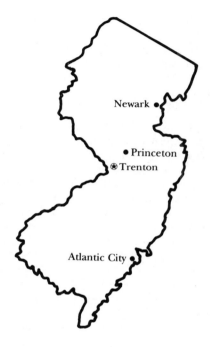

New Jersey, which is almost completely surrounded by water, is one of the original thirteen states. Its capital is Trenton, and Newark is the largest city. Newark is also home to a major international airport.

New Jersey is a manufacturing state, and products include chemicals, clothing, and machinery. Central and southern New Jersey are heavily agricultural, producing primarily field crops such as tomatoes, beets, potatoes, and grapes; livestock is raised in the northern counties. With its many miles of coastline, tourism and water sports play an increasing role in the state's economy. Most of the coastal resorts have some version of the boardwalk concept pioneered by Atlantic City, although that area has revitalized itself through the introduction of casino gambling. Of interest to many visitors is the Edison complex in West Orange.

College Accommodations

Westminster Choir College
Princeton, NJ 08540

Rooms available: May and part of August (call for availability)
Rates: To be determined when present renovation is completed
Facilities: Cafeteria
Policy on children: Accepted
Notes: Small, attractive campus with redbrick Georgian-style buildings
Telephone: 609-921-7101

Westminster Choir College was established in 1926 as a private music college. The 22-acre suburban campus is located in Princeton, about 50 miles from both Philadelphia and New York City.

Princeton (population 12,000) was settled in the 1600s and was known as "Sting Brook" until 1724. There are a number of schools in the town, including Princeton University. Several important battles of the Revolutionary War were fought here, and the Continental Congress met at Nassau Hall in 1783. Palmer Square, a civic center on Nassau Street, has many buildings in a variety of historic styles. Princeton is the birthplace of Paul Robeson and was home to Albert Einstein for his last twenty years. Rockingham State Historic Site, which served as Washington's headquarters, is in the immediate area.

NEW MEXICO
Land of Enchantment
state flower: yucca; state bird: roadrunner

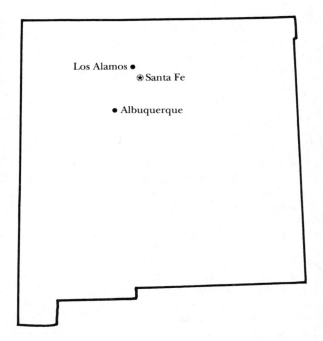

Admitted to the Union in 1912, New Mexico is the forty-seventh state. Its largest city is Albuquerque; Santa Fe is the capital. The state's arid terrain contributed to making ranching the prime industry, although, in the public mind, New Mexico is perhaps most closely associated with the development of the atom bomb at the government-built city of Los Alamos and the testing of the bomb at White Sands.

New Mexico is a tourist's delight. It has clean, dry air, many national parks, and such charming cities as Santa Fe, with its classical Spanish architecture and first-class outdoor opera, and Taos, a writers' and artists' colony and base for winter skiers.

College of Santa Fe
Santa Fe, NM 87501

Rooms available: Mid-May to mid-August
Rates: $18 single; $14 double
Facilities: Cafeteria, laundry, shared bathrooms, soccer, volleyball, campus theater
Policy on children: Children over 5 accepted
Notes: A movie production soundstage, theater, and library are being built here by Greer Garson and her husband
Telephone: 505-473-6270

The College of Santa Fe was established by the Christian Brothers in 1947 as a Catholic college. The 187-acre campus is situated in the foothills of the Sangre de Cristo Mountains about 2 miles from the center of Santa Fe.

Santa Fe is a major cultural center and the oldest state capital in the United States. It has 50,000 inhabitants, and adobe and territorial architecture line the narrow, winding streets, giving the city the distinctive natural charm and atmosphere it has enjoyed since its founding in 1610.

A leading Catholic center, Santa Fe has among its points of interest San Miguel Mission Church (1636), the Cathedral of St. Francis (1869), and the Rey Church, the largest adobe building in the country. The Palace of the Governors, dating from 1610 and occupied in turn by Spanish, Indian, Mexican, and American administrators, is of interest, as are the many arts and crafts shops. Santa Fe is home to a world-famous opera company, and its museum and art galleries reflect its standing as an arts center.

NEW YORK
The Empire State
state flower: rose; state bird: eastern bluebird

One of the original thirteen states, New York stretches from the Atlantic Ocean to the Great Lakes and has ports on both sides, the major ones being in New York City on the Atlantic and Buffalo on Lake Erie.

Both agriculture and manufacturing are important in the state. Rochester is famous for camera and film manufacture and the Kodak Museum; Long Island is known for the manufacture of aircraft and aircraft parts; and the "Big Apple" is a world center of garment manufacture, finance, and theater. Lake Placid, with its Olympic Village, and the Catskill and Adirondack mountains are major sports and recreation areas.

State University of New York at Albany
Albany, NY 12222

Rooms available: Second week in June to mid-August
Rates: Approximately $25 per person
Facilities: Cafeteria facilities not available on weekends

State University of New York at Albany (continued)
Policy on children: Children over 12 accepted
Telephone: 518-442-5435

Founded in 1844, the 382-acre campus of SUNY at Albany is located in a suburban area on the western edge of the city.

Albany has 100,000 residents and is the capital of New York. It is located on the west bank of the Hudson River. The state capitol building, in chateau style, dominates the city. There are many historic buildings, museums, educational institutions, and a new civic center complex. Nearby are Lake George and the Saratoga Battlefield site.

Fordham University
Bronx, NY 10458

Rooms available: June to third week in August
Rates: Variable, depending on type of accommodation
Facilities: Cafeteria, shared bathrooms, pool, racquetball
Policy on children: Accepted
Telephone: 212-579-2325

Fordham University, founded as St. John's College in 1844, is a Jesuit institution. It is located on picturesque Rose Hill, and great care has been taken to preserve its neo-Gothic architecture. Located in New York City, it is close to the New York Botanical Gardens and the Bronx Zoo.

Canisius College
Buffalo, NY 14208

Rooms available: First week in July to third week in August
Rates: $15 single; $20 double
Facilities: Cafeteria, open only for lunch weekdays; Koessler Athletic Center and computer center available to visitors by arrangement
Policy on children: Accepted
Telephone: 716-888-2180

Canisius College was founded in 1879 as a Catholic school but is now a private liberal arts school in the Jesuit tradition. It has a 19-acre campus located within the city limits of Buffalo. Among its facilities are a sports center and a computer center.

Buffalo, a city of 357,000, is on the shores of Lake Erie at the confluence of the Niagara and Buffalo rivers. It is a port of entry and one of the largest grain distribution centers in the country. Places to visit include the Albright-Knox Art Gallery, the Buffalo Museum of Science, the County Historical Society, and the Buffalo Zoological Gardens. The Peace River Bridge connects Buffalo with Fort Erie, Canada, and the Niagara Falls are nearby.

State University of New York College of Technology at Delhi
Delhi, NY 13753

Rooms available: June 1 to first week in August
Rates: $18 single; $12 double
Facilities: Cafeteria, tennis, bowling, track
Restrictions: No pets
Notes: The residences are currently being renovated; inquire for availability
Telephone: 607-746-4162

The College of Technology at Delhi is one of sixty-four colleges in the State University of New York System. Nearby are the Baseball Hall of Fame and the Frisbee Museum. Hanford Museum is about 5 miles distant and the Joseph Burroughs Estate about 35 miles away.

Houghton College
Houghton, NY 14744

Rooms available: June through mid-August
Rates: $9 per person
Facilities: Cafeteria, laundry, kitchenettes, store, some private bathrooms, Olympic-size pool, many sports facilities
Policy on children: Accepted
Restrictions: No tobacco, drugs, alcohol permitted on campus
Telephone: 716-567-2577

Houghton College was established in 1883 and is a small college run under the auspices of the Wesleyan Church of

College Accommodations

Houghton College (continued)
America. Its Wesley Chapel features a 3,153-pipe organ and a 150-foot biblical mural. The 1,250-acre campus is located in a rural area about 60 miles southeast of Buffalo and 65 miles southwest of Rochester.

The rolling hills of the area are rich in Indian and Colonial history, and there are also parks, waterfalls, and a nature conservancy. Letchworth State Park is 14 miles north of the campus. Within easy commuting distance are the Corning Glass Center, Niagara Falls, and Eastman Kodak, with its photo museum and tours.

NEW YORK

With a population of 7 million, New York is the largest city in America and one of the three largest in the world. It consists of five boroughs: Manhattan, the Bronx, Queens, Brooklyn, and Staten Island. The forebears of many Americans entered through the city's Ellis Island.

New York is a major communications center, housing both broadcasting headquarters and publishing enterprises. It is also a leading cultural and educational center. World-famous stores, restaurants, theaters, museums, gardens, architecture, and ethnic neighborhoods combine to make a visit there memorable.

Of special interest for tourists are Chinatown, Fifth Avenue and its shops, Lincoln Center, Central Park, Riverside Drive, Grant's Tomb, Rockefeller Center, the World Trade Center, the Statue of Liberty, the Metropolitan Museum of Art, the Museum of Modern Art, the Guggenheim Museum, and the Whitney Museum of American Art. Broadway and off-Broadway shows are also an attraction.

Fashion Institute of Technology
New York, NY 10001

Rooms available: Mid-June to end of July
Rates: $15 per person; $6 service charge for blanket and

pillow for entire period (no linens provided; minimum 1-week stay)
Facilities: Laundry room
Policy on children: Accepted
Restrictions: No cooking (contact Institute for other rules)
Notes: Exhibits and summer courses available
Telephone: 212-760-7885

The Fashion Institute is a publicly controlled college occupying over a block in the garment district of midtown Manhattan. The Design Center houses a collection of works by craftsmen and artists from around the world, as well as a restoration lab, an indexed collection of clothing and accessories, and more than a million fabric swatches.

Union Theological Seminary
New York, NY 10027

Rooms available: All year (reservations essential)
Rates: $75 single; $100 double
Facilities: Private baths, color TV in each room; all rooms completely refurbished; continental breakfast is only meal available
Policy on children: Accepted from June to mid-August only
Telephone: 212-662-7100

Housed in a building that is listed in the National Register of Historic Places, Union Theological Seminary is located in one of the most exciting urban environments in the world.

YMCAs

In addition to the colleges listed, there are a number of Ys available in New York City. All are open year-round and offer reasonably priced city tours of from three to six days.

College Accommodations

McBurney Y
215 West 23rd Street
New York, NY 10011

Rates: $27 single; $38 double
Facilities: Shared bathrooms, fitness center, swimming pool
Telephone: 212-741-9226

The Vanderbilt Y
224 East 47th Street
New York, NY 10017

Rates: $27 single, $38 double; optional air-conditioning in summer at additional cost
Facilities: Cafeteria, shared bathrooms, pool, fitness center
Telephone: 212-755-2410

West Side Y
5 West 63rd Street
New York, NY 10023

Rates: $27 single; $38 double
Facilities: Cafeteria, shared bathrooms, fitness center
Telephone: 212-787-4400

William Sloane House Y
356 West 34th Street
New York, NY 10001

Rates: $27 single; $38 double
Facilities: Cafeteria, shared bathrooms, fitness center
Telephone: 212-760-5860

Manhattanville College
Purchase, NY 10577

Rooms available: Third week in May to third week in August

Rates: Approximately $15 (2-week minimum stay)
Facilities: Cafeteria available part of the summer, swimming pool, running track
Telephone: 914-694-2200

Manhattanville College was established in 1841 as an independent college operated by the Religious of the Sacred Heart. The 220-acre campus is located in Westchester County, adjacent to White Plains and about 30 miles from New York City. The College's nineteenth-century castle is a historic landmark.

Westchester County retains much of its past elegance, with wooded areas and winding country roads. Elijah Miller's House, used by George Washington during the Battle of White Plains, and the White Plains Battlefield itself are items of interest for history buffs.

Wagner College
Staten Island, NY 10301-4495

Rooms available: All year (reservations required)
Rates: $20 per person
Facilities: Cafeteria, laundry, store, shared bathrooms, all sports
Policy on children: Accepted
Notes: Theater, art gallery, concerts on campus
Telephone: 718-390-3221

Wagner College is affiliated with the United Lutheran Church. It was established in 1883 and occupies an 86-acre campus on a hill overlooking New York Harbor and the Atlantic Ocean. It offers a spectacular view of Manhattan and the Verrazano Bridge. The Statue of Liberty and the various cultural and shopping facilities of the city are readily available.

College Accommodations

NORTH CAROLINA
The Tarheel State
state flower: dogwood; state bird: cardinal

North Carolina is one of the original thirteen colonies; its capital is Raleigh, and other prominent cities are Charlotte, Greensboro, and Winston-Salem. North Carolina is a leading producer of tobacco, textiles, furniture, and such minerals and metals as feldspar, mica, and lithium. Its Atlantic coast makes fishing an important industry, and the many sandbars create beaches that are attractive to tourists. The Blue Ridge and Great Smoky mountains also appeal to those who enjoy the outdoors.

The Wright Brothers' historic manned flight took place at Kitty Hawk, now a national park. Several Civil War battlefields and a memorial to the poet Carl Sandburg are also of interest.

University of North Carolina at Chapel Hill
Chapel Hill, NC 27514

Rooms available: Third week in May to first week in August (reservations required)

Rates: $16 per day, $96 per week, single; $11 per person per day, $60 per person per week, double

Facilities: Cafeteria, shared bathrooms, library, swimming pool, gym

Policy on children: Accepted

Telephone: 919-966-5966

The University was established in 1795 and is the oldest state university in the country. The 1,200-acre campus is located 30 miles from Raleigh in an urban setting.

Chapel Hill (population 25,000) is the cultural center of the Southeast. Facilities include Moorehead Planetarium, Ackland Art Museum, and the North Carolina Botanical Gardens.

Raleigh, the state capital, has museums, a theater, and a number of eighteenth-century houses, including the birthplace of Andrew Jackson.

Greensboro College
Greensboro, NC 27401

Rooms available: All year (reservations required)
Rates: $15 single; $20 double
Facilities: Cafeteria, laundry, kitchenettes, store, some private bathrooms
Policy on children: Accepted
Telephone: 919-272-7102

Greensboro College was chartered in 1838 as the only women's college in North Carolina; it is the third-oldest in the country. A small liberal arts college, it is affiliated with the Methodist Church. The 30-acre campus is in a suburban area, near the City Square.

Greensboro (population 160,000) is the second-largest city in North Carolina. It has an important textile industry and is a financial, insurance, and distribution center for the region. The Eastern Music Festival is held here each summer, and the Greensboro Historical Museum and the Masonic Temple Museum are of interest. Both Dolley Madison and O. Henry were born here, and the nearby site of the Revolutionary War battle of Guilford Courthouse is now a National Military Park. Other points of interest in the area include Old Salem and the North Carolina Zoo.

College Accommodations

NORTH DAKOTA
The Peace Garden State
state flower: wild prairie rose; state bird: western meadowlark

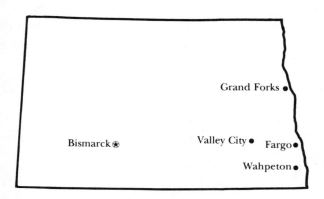

North Dakota, the thirty-ninth state, was admitted to the Union with South Dakota in 1889. Its capital is Bismarck; Minot, Grand Forks, and Fargo are small but important cities.

Most of North Dakota's population is engaged in farming or providing services to farmers. However, the western part of the state, too hilly and barren to produce crops, is devoted to the raising of cattle. Oil and petroleum products and coal are also mainstays of the North Dakota economy. Fishing, boating, and hunting are leading vacation sports, and the state parks are popular.

Valley City State University
Valley City, ND 58072

Rooms available: Summer only, for such groups as family reunions
Rates: Call for prices and availability
Telephone: 701-845-7412

Valley City State is a four-year coeducational college founded in 1890. It has a campus of 55 acres.

Valley City, which is a small city of some 7,500 inhabitants, is the site of Baldhill Dam on the Sheyenne River. The dam created Lake Ashtabula, some 27 miles long, and is also the site of the Sheyenne Valley Recreational Complex, where swimming, fishing, and water sports are available.

North Dakota State College of Science
Wahpeton, ND 58075

Rooms available: June to mid-August
Rates: $10 per person
Facilities: Cafeteria available weekdays only
Restrictions: Group bookings only
Telephone: 701-671-2194

Wahpeton, a small town of 10,000 persons, is located at the headwaters of the Bois and Sioux rivers. The Richland County Historical Museum is open during June, July, and August. Chahinpaka Park, on the state border, covers about 45 acres and includes a swimming pool and a golf course with nine holes in North Dakota and nine in Minnesota.

College Accommodations

OHIO
The Buckeye State
state flower: red carnation; state bird: cardinal

Ohio was admitted to the Union as the seventeenth state in 1803. Its capital is Columbus, and its other important cities are Cleveland, Cincinnati, Toledo, and Akron. Although chiefly an industrial state and the major producer of limestone in the country, Ohio also has much agriculture, with corn and soybeans important among the many crops. Manufactured goods range from steel, auto parts, and transportation equipment to plastic and rubber goods. Prominent industrial-research firms in Columbus and Cleveland complement rubber-research companies in Akron.

There are major symphonies in Cleveland and Cincinnati, and Columbus is well known for its jazz musicians. With Lake Erie in the north and many smaller lakes, fishing, swimming, and water sports are popular.

Ohio University
Athens, OH 45701

Rooms available: End of June until late summer (reservations required)
Rates: Approximately $9 per person
Facilities: Cafeteria, shared bathrooms, aquatic and athletic center, golf course
Policy on children: Accepted, under adult supervision
Telephone: 614-593-4086 Reservations

Founded in 1804, Ohio University is located on 641 rural acres in the town of Athens, 30 miles south of Lancaster and 75 miles southeast of Columbus. The Anthony G. Trisolene Gallery, located in an early Athens mansion on campus, has regular exhibits. Cutler Hall, completed in 1816, is the oldest college building west of the Allegheny Mountains and was declared a National Historic Landmark in 1956.

At Nelsonville, just north of Athens, is the Hocking Valley Scenic Railroad, which provides a 12-mile round-trip using a 1916 steam engine. Some 18 miles from Athens, Hocking Hill State Park has much of interest to nature lovers. Additional attractions in the area include Ash Cave, Cantwell Cliffs, Cedar Falls, Ginkler Hollow, Old Man's Cave and Rock House, and Strouds Run Park and Dairy Barn Art Exhibit. Lancaster is noted for the Sherman House Memorial, birthplace of William T. Sherman, while Columbus has its museums and German Village.

CINCINNATI

A city of some 500,000 inhabitants, Cincinnati is the third-largest city in Ohio and is an industrial, commercial, and cultural center. It is the birthplace of William Howard Taft and his son Robert, known as "Mr. Republican." Cincinnati's landmarks include the Taft Museum, Eden Park with its art museum, the zoo, and the stadium. The Cincinnati Fire Museum features restored fire fighting equipment from other days.

The downtown area has been rebuilt around Fountain Square, which sits above a large underground garage. Skywalks are extensively used to

Cincinnati (continued)
connect buildings in the area. Ballet, opera, a first-rate symphony orchestra, and various festivals combine to make the city a vital and interesting place.

College of Mount St. Joseph
Cincinnati, OH 45051

Rooms available: All year (reservations required)
Rates: $15 single; $20 double
Facilities: Cafeteria, laundry, store, some private bathrooms, indoor swimming pool, tennis, volleyball, pool table, theater, chapel, space for strolling and jogging
Policy on children: Conditionally accepted
Telephone: 513-244-4373

The College, which was founded in 1923, is a Catholic institution operated by the Sisters of Charity. The 250-acre campus overlooks the Ohio River in a suburban area 5 miles from downtown Cincinnati.

University of Cincinnati
Cincinnati, OH 45218

Rooms available: Mid-June to end of August
Rates: Group rates begin at $10 per person; individual rates on request
Facilities: Cafeteria, laundry, kitchenettes, some private bathrooms, theater
Policy on children: Accepted
Telephone: 513-556-0682

Located 2 miles from downtown Cincinnati, the University, which was founded in 1819, has an enrollment of about 36,000. The campus is in a scenic setting and features historic architecture.

Hiram College
Hiram, OH 44234

Rooms available: All year
Rates: $15 single; $25 double
Facilities: Cafeteria, restaurant

Policy on children: Accepted
Notes: Visitors have access to most campus activities during the school year
Telephone: 216-569-5232

Hiram College was founded in 1850 as a private nonsectarian college related to the Christian Church. The 145-acre campus is located in a small village in the beautiful rolling countryside of northeast Ohio, within 35 miles of Akron, Cleveland, Canton, and Youngstown. Nearby are Sea World, Gauga Lake Park, and the professional sports of Cleveland.

Akron is noted for a giant dirigible airdock, one of the world's largest buildings without inner supports. It also has several old mansions, among them the John Brown House, where the abolitionist lived from 1844 to 1846. The McKinley Museum is in Canton. Cleveland's points of interest include the Civic Center Mall, the Terminal Tower, several museums, and Severance Hall.

Franciscan University of Steubenville
Steubenville, OH 43952

Rooms available: All year, usually weekdays only (reservations essential)
Rates: $15 per person
Facilities: Cafeteria, shared bathrooms, most outdoor sports
Policy on children: Accepted
Notes: Campus offers a definite Catholic atmosphere
Telephone: 614-283-6314, 800-282-8283

The University occupies a 100-acre campus in Steubenville, about 40 miles west of Pittsburgh, Pennsylvania.

The city of Steubenville has a population of 25,000. It houses the Jefferson County Historical Museum, which has an outstanding genealogical collection, as well as samples of early glass and pottery and a turn-of-the-century kitchen.

University of Toledo
Toledo, OH 43606

Rooms available: June 15 to October 1 (reservations required)

College Accommodations

University of Toledo (continued)
Rates: $9 per person, double
Facilities: Cafeteria, laundry, kitchenettes, shared bathrooms, movie theaters
Policy on children: Accepted
Notes: Walking tour of the campus available
Telephone: 419-537-2941

The University, which was founded in 1872 as a state-assisted school, occupies two campuses totaling some 407 acres in a residential area of western Toledo.

Toledo (population 345,000) is an industrial center and busy freshwater port on Lake Erie. The city has been modernized but offers historic sites in its various parks. One of these, Crosby Gardens, has a fragrance section, a children's garden, and a re-created pioneer home. The Toledo Museum of Art, with its collection of glassware and ancient artifacts, is well worth a visit, as is Portside Festival Marketplace, which offers some seventy specialty shops on the waterfront.

OKLAHOMA
The Sooner State
state flower: mistletoe; state bird: scissortailed flycatcher

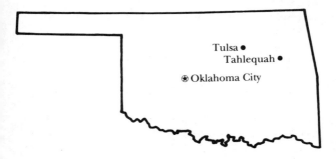

Our forty-sixth state, Oklahoma was admitted to the Union in 1907. Its capital is Oklahoma City, and Tulsa is its second-largest city. Livestock and wheat rank first and second in the state's economy; however, Oklahoma City and Tulsa are better known for their oil production.

The state was first opened for homesteading in 1889. It takes its nickname from the bands of settlers who grabbed up the best parcels of land "sooner" than was allowed by the law. Oil was first drilled in Bartlesville in 1897, and Oklahoma became a major producer by 1904. However, the state went through a boom-and-bust period with its oil, as it did when its agricultural land dried up and the "Okies" were forced to travel west looking for other sites to settle. Flood and erosion control, as well as the limitation of drilling sites, have served to correct many past ills.

The state now has a navigation system that connects it to the Gulf of Mexico. Although it is a prairie state, Oklahoma has several mountain ranges. With about a million acres of lakes and rivers, water sports are important, while hunting is also popular.

Northeastern State University
Tahlequah, OK 74465

Rooms available: June 1 to August 1 (reservations required)
Rates: $10, single; $7 per person, double
Facilities: Cafeteria, laundry, shared bathrooms, fitness center, bowling, tennis, billiards, theater
Policy on children: Accepted
Telephone: 918-456-5511

Northeastern State University was founded by the Cherokee National Council in 1846 following the passage of an act providing for the establishment of a national male seminary and a national female seminary. Seminary Hall, built in 1878, still remains on the campus. The 176-acre campus is nestled in the foothills of the Ozarks at Tahlequah (population 10,000). This is a suburban area 75 miles from Tulsa and 35 miles from Muskogee.

Near Tahlequah are the scenic Illinois River, Lake Tenkiller Ferry, and Lake Fort Gibson, which offer sailing, fishing, swimming, and canoeing. Also of interest are Tsa-La-Gi, a replica of a seventeenth-century Cherokee village; the Cherokee National Museum; and the Trail of Tears, an outdoor drama depicting Cherokee history.

OREGON
The Beaver State
state flower: Oregon grape; state bird: western meadowlark

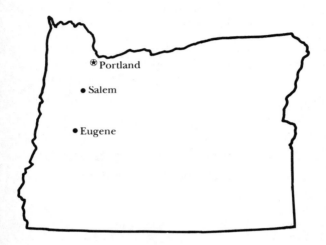

The thirty-third state, Oregon was admitted to the Union in 1859. Its capital is Salem, and other major cities are Portland and Eugene. Lumber and associated products, cattle, wheat, barley, and fishing are important to the Oregon economy, while tourism ranks as a leading industry.

Mountains, lakes, Pacific Ocean beaches, and rich agricultural areas make Oregon a state with much to offer. The rainy coastal area around Portland is balanced by the eastern two thirds of the state, which is cut off from much of the precipitation by the Cascade Range.

Warner Pacific College
Portland, OR 92715

Rooms available: June 15 to September 1
Rates: $5 per person (no linens provided)
Restrictions: No smoking, no drinking, no pets permitted on campus; dorms are separated according to sex
Telephone: 503-775-4366

Warner Pacific College, founded in 1937, is affiliated with the Church of God. The 28-acre campus is located in the heart of Portland adjacent to Mount Tabor Park.

Portland (population 366,000) is Oregon's leading city. It is located on the Columbia River and, despite its distance from the ocean, is Oregon's major port. Scenically situated between the Cascade Mountains to the east and the Coast Range to the west, its great beauty is enhanced by some 150 parks.

Nearby are Multnomah Falls, Mount Hood, and the Pacific coast, while the city itself has the following points of interest: Bybee Howell House, the Children's Museum, the Georgia-Pacific Historical Museum, the Old Church, the Oregon Historical Museum, the Oregon Museum of Science and Industry, and the Portland Art Museum.

PENNSYLVANIA
The Keystone State
state flower: mountain laurel; state bird: ruffed grouse

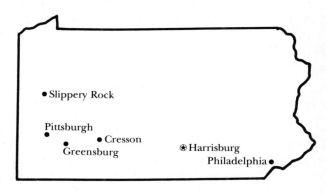

Pennsylvania was one of the original thirteen colonies. Its capital is Harrisburg, which is more or less midway between Philadelphia, on the eastern border, and Pittsburgh, near the western border. There are coastal plains in the northwest and southeast, while the Appalachian and Allegheny mountains and rolling hills give the rest of the state its character. The presence of coal led to steel production, so manufacturing is of major importance, although agriculture plays an important role as well.

The Amish people, or "Pennsylvania Dutch," attract many tourists, as do the historic sites of Gettysburg. The Pittsburgh and Philadelphia orchestras are world-famous, and a visit to Philadelphia's Main Line will show an aspect of life that is fast disappearing. There are many museums featuring early American artifacts in the state.

Mount Aloysius Junior College
Cresson, PA 16330

Rooms available: Approximately mid-May to mid-August (reservations required)
Rates: $10 per person
Facilities: Laundry, kitchenettes, shared bathrooms (2 rooms per bath), sports facilities
Policy on children: Accepted
Telephone: 814-886-4131

The College is an independent Roman Catholic institution founded in 1939. Its 125-acre campus is situated in a scenic rural setting.

Cresson is located some 20 minutes from Johnstown and Altoona. It is a small town of around 2,500 people and is the home of the Allegheny Portage Railroad National Historic Site, which shows some of the old stone railroad ties and the quarry where they were mined. There is a museum in the 1831 Lemon House Tavern that offers a slide show of the history of the railroad. Crafts of the eighteenth century are also displayed in the summer. In the area, there are also state parks, an amusement park, and the Forest Zoo.

Altoona is a railroad town and has various museums dedicated to trains, while Johnstown is famed for having been flooded several times. In addition to the flood museum, Johnstown is notable for the Inclined Plane that connects the center of the town with a residential suburb: it is about 1,000 feet long, has a 71 percent grade, and carries both pedestrians and motor vehicles.

Seton Hill College
Greensburg, PA 15601

Rooms available: Mid-May to end of July
Rates: $10–$20 per person
Facilities: Cafeteria, kitchenettes, store, shared bathrooms, tennis, gym, swimming, volleyball

Policy on children: Accepted
Telephone: 412-834-2200

Seton Hill, established in 1883 by the Catholic Church, is located on a 200-acre campus just 30 miles east of Pittsburgh. It offers an opportunity for a quiet country life within easy reach of a major city. In beautiful surroundings on rolling land, the College has a nineteenth-century chapel and presents frequent theatrical productions.

Greensburg is the county seat. It has a symphony orchestra and a museum.

PHILADELPHIA

The United States was born in Philadelphia with the Declaration of Independence; the Constitution was drafted there. Independence Hall, by today's standards quite tiny, rubs shoulders with the modern steel and glass of Penn Center, and modern ocean liners, instead of the sailing ships of yesteryear, make their way the 70 miles up the Delaware. Cobblestone streets wander among the paved ones, and restored homes on Society Hill and in Germantown stand cheek by jowl with modern ones. The mansions of the Main Line, once on the main line of the Pennsylvania Railroad, still offer sightseers a glimpse of gracious living.

Sites of historic interest include Christ Church, where George Washington, Benjamin Franklin, and Betsy Ross worshiped, and Congress Hall, where the U.S. Congress met from 1790 to 1800 and where George Washington was inaugurated as first President of the United States. Fairmount Park, founded in 1812, offers some 8,500 acres of walking and bridle paths, several old mansions, and horticultural gardens.

La Salle University
Philadelphia, PA 19141

Rooms available: June and July (reservations required)
Rates: $10–$20 per person

La Salle University (continued)

Facilities: Cafeteria, laundry, kitchenettes, store, both private and shared bathrooms, tennis, pool, track
Policy on children: Accepted
Telephone: 215-951-1550

La Salle is a liberal arts college operated under the auspices of the Brothers of the Christian Schools of the Roman Catholic Church. The 95-acre campus is located 6 miles from the center of Philadelphia, a city of about 1.7 million people.

Carlow College
Pittsburgh, PA 15213

Rooms available: All year
Rates: $15 per person per night; $320 per month (weekly and group rates available)
Facilities: Kitchenettes, lounges, color TV
Policy on children: Accepted
Notes: Secure buildings in the cultural center of Pittsburgh, 5 minutes from downtown
Telephone: 412-578-6000

Originally named Mount Mercy College, Carlow is an independent institution, primarily for women, operated by the Sisters of Mercy. The 13-acre campus is in the Oakland district of Pittsburgh.

Pittsburgh, located in the western portion of the state, is a comparatively small city of about 450,000 people, with about 2.25 million in the metropolitan area. At one time it was probably the smokiest place in the country, but now its air is clean and the city has undergone a renaissance that is still in progress.

The city was established by George Washington when he was a major in the British colonial army; it was named after the British statesman William Pitt. The city is built on hilly terrain, with valleys and rivers crossed by many bridges. It is very proud of its various ethnic neighborhoods. Of interest to visitors are the Carnegie Institute, which contains several museums, and the Cathedral of Learning, part of the University of Pittsburgh. Hartwood Acres is a re-creation of an English country estate a square mile in size, while the zoo and children's zoo are also of interest.

Pennsylvania

Point Park College
Pittsburgh, PA 15222

Rooms available: May 1 to August 31
Rates: $12 per person
Facilities: Cafeteria
Restrictions: No children, no pets; guests must be members of the American Youth Hostel Association
Telephone: 412-391-4100

Point Park College was founded in 1960 and is an independent school occupying three high-rise buildings in the downtown area. Immediately accessible to the school are the Civic Arena, Station Square, the Carnegie Institute, and Point State Park.

Slippery Rock University of Pennsylvania
Slippery Rock, PA 16057

Rooms available: Third week in May to second week in August (reservations required)
Rates: $12 single; $7.50 per person, double
Facilities: Cafeteria, laundry, kitchenettes, ministore, shared bathrooms, tennis, swimming
Policy on children: Accepted
Telephone: 412-794-7551

Slippery Rock was founded in 1838 and is controlled by the commonwealth of Pennsylvania. The 620-acre campus is located in a rural area some 50 miles north of Pittsburgh.

Nearby points of interest include Moraine State Park; Drake Oil Well, reputed to be the first producing oil well in the country; Jennings Nature Reserve; and the Old Stone House.

College Accommodations

SOUTH DAKOTA
The Coyote State
state flower: pasque flower; state bird: ringnecked pheasant

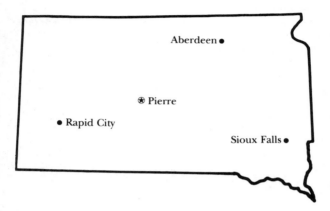

The fortieth state, South Dakota was admitted to the Union with North Dakota in 1889. Its major cities are Sioux Falls, Rapid City, and Aberdeen, while the capital is Pierre. Livestock, corn, and wheat are the main crops, and food processing and meat packing are the main occupations of the residents. Gold and beryllium concentrate are found here. The town of Lead, center of the mining area, is located in the Black Hills.

Some of the oldest rock known to man has been discovered in the Black Hills and the Badlands. Mount Rushmore, with its world-famous presidential sculptures, is in South Dakota.

Northern State College
Aberdeen, SD 57401

Rooms available: June 1 to August 1
Rates: $9 single; $6 per person, double; linens $2
Facilities: Cafeteria, tennis courts
Policy on children: Accepted
Restrictions: No alcohol
Telephone: 605-622-2530

Northern State was founded in 1901 and occupies 50 acres within the city of Aberdeen.

Aberdeen (population 26,000) is unusual in the farm belt in having many trees. Most of the trees were planted by homesick settlers trying to make the city look like the forested eastern states from which they had come. As a result, the town is quite attractive. Frank Baum, author of *The Wizard of Oz*, lived in Aberdeen.

National College
Rapid City, SD 57701

Rooms available: June through August (reservations required)
Rates: $14–$24, depending on number in party (each room accommodates 5)
Facilities: Cafeteria, laundry, both shared and private bathrooms, outdoor swimming pool
Policy on children: Accepted
Telephone: 605-394-4978

National College was founded in 1841 and is located in a suburban area of Rapid City.

Rapid City (population 46,000) was founded in 1876 after gold was discovered in the nearby Black Hills. The hills were so named by the Indians because they appeared dark as a result of a thick covering of pine trees. Mining and lumbering are the major industries in the area, and Rapid City is now a trucking and tourist center for the region.

Travelers enjoy attending the auto racing and greyhound racing that take place in summer, as well as visiting the Black Hills Caverns, Richmond Ghost Town, and Custer State Park.

TENNESSEE
The Volunteer State
state flower: iris; state bird: mockingbird

Tennessee, the sixteenth state, was admitted to the Union in 1796. The capital, Nashville, is second in size to Memphis; Knoxville, Chattanooga, and Oak Ridge are other important cities.

The Tennessee Valley Authority, a source of controversy since its inception in the 1930s, provides power to the entire area. Long famous for tobacco and horses, Tennessee is now largely supported by manufacturing, especially of electrical machinery and glass, and mining, particularly of stone, zinc, and pyrites.

The terrain is primarily rolling hills, with the Appalachian and Great Smoky mountains in the east. Although there are several national parks worth visiting, Mud Island in the Mississippi River off Memphis offers a chance to see the mighty waterway both in real life and in model form.

University of Tennessee, Knoxville
Knoxville, TN 37996

Rooms available: Mid-June to mid-September
Rates: $19 single; $17 per person, double; $2 linen charge
Facilities: Cafeteria, numerous campus activities
Policy on children: Accepted
Notes: Visitors must have an educationally related purpose
Telephone: 615-974-2571

The University was founded in 1794 and occupies 1,000 acres on the banks of the Tennessee River about a mile from downtown Knoxville.

Knoxville (population 183,000) was the site of the 1982 World's Fair, and the fair area is being converted into a permanent recreation area. The downtown area has been revitalized with hotels, plazas, and government buildings. Confederate Memorial Hall, the Dublin Gallery of Art, the McClung Museum, Governor Blount House, James White's Fort, and the zoo are among Knoxville's places of interest. Great Smoky Mountains National Park, Oak Ridge National Laboratory, and the resort town of Gatlinburg are all quite close.

Middle Tennessee State University
Murfreesboro, TN 37132

Rooms available: Third week in May to first week in August (reservations required)
Rates: $9 per person per night, double; $40 per week, double; linens and towels, $7 per pack per person (no blankets)
Facilities: Cafeteria, laundry, shared bathrooms
Policy on children: Conditionally accepted
Restrictions: No alcoholic beverages on campus
Telephone: 615-898-2860

Middle Tennessee State was founded in 1911, and its 600-acre campus is located in the heart of the state, 32 miles from Nashville.

Murfreesboro (population 33,000) was the state capital from 1810 to 1835 and has several historic sites, including the Rutherford County Courthouse; Cannonsburgh, a reconstruction of early southern life; and Oakland's Mansions. There are bike trails linking battlefield sites in the area, as well as a number of monuments of historic interest.

Fisk University
Nashville, TN 37203

Rooms available: Facilities are currently being renovated (1989); call for dates of availability and prices
Telephone: 615-329-8598

Fisk is a private, nonsectarian university affiliated with the American Missionary Association. It was established in 1856 as a college for black students.

Fisk University (continued)

Nashville (population 456,000) was founded on Christmas Day 1799. It was the home of Andrew Jackson, James Polk, and General Sam Houston. Nashville is well known for Music City, the Country Music Hall of Fame, Opryland, and the Grand Old Opry. Historic mansions in the area include Belle Meade, Belmont, and the Hermitage. Also of interest are the Cumberland Museum and Science Center, the Tennessee State Museum, the Country Music Stars Museum, Fort Nashborough, the Parthenon, Ryan Auditorium, and the Tennessee Game Farm Zoo.

TEXAS
The Lone Star State
state flower: bluebonnet; state bird: mockingbird

Admitted to the Union in 1845, Texas was the twenty-eighth state. Its capital is Austin and its largest cities are Houston, Dallas, and San Antonio.

Texas is so big that it encompasses entirely different zones. The eastern portion is typically southern, with pine-covered hills, cypress swamps, and the remains of cotton plantations; oil and petroleum products and Houston's space center and ship canal contribute to the industrial side of the region. The southern portion is known for citrus and winter vegetable production. The western and northern areas are heavily agricultural, with oil and cattle also of importance. Since the state shares a thousand-mile border with Mexico, many of its cities have a strong Spanish presence.

Bauder Fashion College
Arlington, TX 76101

Rooms available: June, July, and August (reservations preferred)
Rates: Approximately $22.50 single; $12.50 per person, double
Facilities: Laundry, kitchenettes, TV, air-conditioned rooms with private bathrooms, swimming pool
Policy on children: Accepted
Telephone: 817-277-6666

Bauder Fashion College is located in Arlington, an industrial city of some 215,000 about 14 miles from Fort Worth and 21 miles from Dallas.

Six Flags over Texas, a giant amusement park, and the Pecan Bowl are located in Arlington, but the city's major growth came with the construction of a General Motors plant in 1954.

Texas Woman's University
Denton, TX 76204

Rooms available: Mid-July to mid-August (reservations required)
Rates: $16 single; $11 per person, double
Facilities: Cafeteria, laundry, private bathrooms, tennis, 18-hole golf course, campus theater
Policy on children: Those over 12 accepted
Restrictions: Visitors should have educationally related purposes
Telephone: 817-898-3682

Texas Woman's University is a state school established in 1901. The 270-acre campus is located in a suburban area of

Texas Woman's University (continued)

Denton, a city of 50,000 some 35 miles from the Dallas area. Denton is in a beautiful, tree-laden region and enjoys a country atmosphere. It has museums, an art council, and, of course, a shopping mall, and it is close enough to Dallas to take advantage of the various cultural activities there.

University of Texas at El Paso
El Paso, TX 79968

Rooms available: May to September (reservations required)
Rates: $8 single; $4 per person, double; $10 per person, private room; linens $3 per person
Facilities: Cafeteria, kitchenettes, shared bathrooms, pool, tennis, game room
Policy on children: Accepted at adult rate
Restrictions: No cooking in rooms, no alcoholic beverages
Telephone: 915-742-5352 (weekdays 9 to 5 for reservations)

Established in 1913 as the Texas State School of Mines, the University of Texas at El Paso occupies 333 acres. The campus is in a beautifully rugged mountain setting, where the Rio Grande cuts through the foothills of the southernmost Rockies.

The historic contributions of many cultures form a four-century backdrop to life in this region. El Paso (population 425,000) was founded in 1682 and is the oldest city in Texas. Its Spanish name was Misión Nuestra Señora del Carmen. The Ysleta Mission was built around 1682 by Tigua Indians, and it, as well as the original Señora Mission, are still in everyday use; both blend Spanish and Indian architecture. Placito Santa Fe, El Paso's old town, houses many shops and galleries. There is much to see, including the Bullfight Museum, the Chamizal National Memorial, and the El Paso Museum of Art and History. The El Paso area is one of the few where long-staple Egyptian cotton is grown.

Texas

Sam Houston State University
Huntsville, TX 77341

Rooms available: End of May to mid-August (reservations required)
Rates: $6 single; $9 double (no linens provided)
Facilities: Cafeteria, swimming pool, tennis courts
Policy on children: Accepted
Restrictions: No cooking, no pets in room
Telephone: 409-294-1810

Sam Houston State, established in 1879, is a publicly supported institution. The 160-acre campus is located in pine forests in a rural environment in southeast Texas, some 60 miles from Houston.

Huntsville, a city of 25,000, has a blending of old and new, beauty and bustle, serenity and activity. On its outskirts is the Sam Houston Museum and Park, with Sam Houston's house, built in 1847, and the Steamboat House, where he died. On the park's grounds are Houston's law office, a memorial museum, and period artifacts. Nearby are Huntsville State Park, Lake Livingston, and the cities of Houston and Galveston.

SAN ANTONIO

A city of about 650,000 in south-central Texas, San Antonio is known as the cradle of Texas independence. It is the home of the Alamo, built in 1744 as a Franciscan mission, where in 1836 some 180 defenders fought an army of 5,000 Mexicans to the death. "Remember the Alamo" became a rallying cry for Texans.

A very pretty city, San Antonio has merged old Spanish architecture with modern skyscrapers. Of interest are La Villeta, a 250-year-old settlement; Paseo del Río, a charming river walk, the Governor's Palace, and San José Mission National Historic Site.

College Accommodations

Bullis House
621 Pierce Street
San Antonio, TX 78206

Rooms available: All year
Rates: $23 single ($40 with private bath); $27 double ($40 with private bath)
Telephone: 512-436-3714

Located in an international hostel, Bullis House provides travelers with an opportunity to sightsee in San Antonio.

St. Mary's University of San Antonio
San Antonio, TX 78284

Rooms available: Second week in May to mid-August (reservations preferred)
Rates: Variable, depending on type of accommodation
Facilities: Cafeteria, laundry, kitchenettes, store, both private and shared bathrooms, swimming, tennis, volleyball, basketball, jogging
Policy on children: Accepted
Telephone: 512-436-3714

St. Mary's is a Catholic school, founded in 1852. It consists of 125 acres in a suburban area 5 miles north of downtown San Antonio and has chapels, cathedrals, a pecan grove, a quad, and courtyards.

VERMONT
The Green Mountain State
state flower: red clover; state bird: hermit thrush

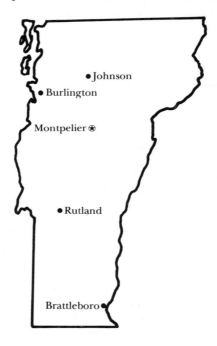

The state's nickname is actually a translation from the French "vert mont." The fourteenth state, Vermont was for a time an independent republic, issuing its own money and postage and appointing ambassadors to foreign governments. It might have been one of the original states, except that it was embroiled in a border dispute with New York that kept it from becoming a state until New York withdrew its land claims.

The capital of Vermont is Montpelier, but Burlington, with a population of around 40,000, is the largest city. Agriculture, manufacturing, and tourism are of importance in the state, with water sports, skiing, and mountaineering the most popular pastimes. Naturally Vermont has its Green Mountains and Green Mountain State Forest.

College Accommodations

Johnson State College
Johnson, VT 05656

Rooms available: Summer
Rates: Approximately $15 (call for current rates)
Facilities: Cafeteria, shared bathrooms, laundry, tennis, hiking, films, concerts, museum
Policy on children: Accepted
Notes: Rooms rented primarily to conferences, but open to public on a space-available basis
Telephone: 802-635-2356

Johnson State is a public college founded in 1828. The 500-acre campus is in a rural setting on a hilltop overlooking the village of Johnson, which is located in the heart of the Vermont ski country.

The nearest large cities are Burlington and Montpelier, each about 5 miles away. Montpelier has a population of about 8,500 and is an insurance center and the site of granite quarrying. The Supreme Court building, open to the public, is made of Barre granite. The State Historical Building and the Thomas W. Wood Art Gallery are also of interest to visitors.

Burlington (population 40,000) is the largest city in Vermont. It is an industrial and trading center, founded in 1773. A port of entry located on Lake Champlain, it is the burial place of Ethan Allen. Battery Park, the site of battles between American and British forces in the War of 1812, and the Robert Hull Fleming Museum are worth a visit.

College of St. Joseph
Rutland, VT, 05701

Rooms available: June through mid-August
Rates: Very reasonable; call for current rates
Facilities: Cafeteria, sports facilities
Telephone: 802-773-5900

St. Joseph was established as an independent college affiliated with the Sisters of St. Joseph in 1954. The 99-acre campus is located 1 mile north of Rutland and 160 miles from Boston.

With a population of around 19,000, Rutland has been nicknamed "the Marble City" because of its quarries and the marble finishing carried on there. Located in the Otter Creek Valley, it is protected by the Taconic Mountains to the west and the Green Mountains to the east. It is the headquarters for the Green Mountain National Forest and is near the Norman Rockwell Museum.

VIRGINIA
The Old Dominion
state flower: dogwood; state bird: cardinal

Virginia was the first state of the original thirteen to ratify the Constitution. Its capital is at Richmond, and Norfolk is the largest city. Virginia is a neighbor of the District of Columbia, and Arlington and Alexandria are important cities in the federal establishment.

The state, which has coastal plains, rolling fertile land, and mountains, ranks agriculture as its number one money-maker. Crops include tobacco, peanuts, and apples. Fishing is important, while the state also gains financially from the naval shipyard at Portsmouth.

Tourists will find much of historic interest in Virginia, especially restored Williamsburg, one of the oldest American cities. The state is home to such diverse attractions as Thomas Jefferson's home, Monticello, surprising in its relative modernity; Mount Vernon, where visitors can sit on rocking chairs on the porch overlooking the Potomac and pretend to be visiting George Washington; an assortment of battlefields dating from both the War of Independence and the War Between the States; various shipyards and military establishments; and historic cities like Williamsburg, Jamestown, and Fredericksburg.

College Accommodations

Alexandria/Washington Y
420 East Monroe Avenue
Alexandria, VA 22301

Rooms available: All year
Rates: $28 single; $30 double
Facilities: Shared bathrooms, fitness center, swimming pool
Notes: 3- to 5-day package tours available
Telephone: 703-549-0850

This is one of two Ys serving the Washington, D.C., area. It is located just a few miles from the city and offers an excellent opportunity to see both Alexandria and Washington.

Marymount University
Arlington, VA 22207

Rooms available: Mid-May to first week in August
Rates: $20 single; $36.60 double
Facilities: Cafeteria, gym, swimming pool, hockey field
Policy on children: Accepted
Telephone: 703-284-1540

Marymount is affiliated with the Catholic Church and is located in a suburban area about 7 miles from Washington, D.C. The campus was formerly the estate of P. M. Rixey, surgeon general of the Navy and personal physician to President McKinley and Teddy Roosevelt.

Arlington, a city of 175,000, is situated across the Potomac River from Washington. It was ceded to the federal government in 1790 and was part of the District of Columbia until 1843, when it was returned to Virginia. It is the home of Arlington National Cemetery, burial place of several Presidents and location of the Tomb of the Unknown Soldier. Arlington also features the Greek Revival home of Robert E. Lee. Nearby is Fairfax, a historic treasure trove. A few miles from the college is Manassus National Park, site of the Battle of Bull Run, one of the major engagements of the Civil War. The audiovisual presentation at the Battlefield Museum is memorable.

University of Virginia
Charlottesville, VA 22904

Notes: Residence facilities are open primarily to those on University business; however, those with specific educational interests may inquire about space availability

Telephone: 804-924-3314 (Director of Conference Services)

The University was formed in 1819 by Thomas Jefferson, who planned its early curriculum as well as the grounds and original buildings. It is located in Charlottesville, 70 miles from Richmond and 110 miles from Washington, D.C.

Historic Charlottesville (population 45,000) is in the foothills of the Blue Ridge Mountains. It was the home of Thomas Jefferson and James Monroe. Both the town and surrounding countryside have many estates that reflect Jefferson's architecture.

There is easy access from Charlottesville to Monticello and Ash Lawn, as well as the Michie Tavern Museum, the Lewis and Clark Memorial, Shenandoah National Park, and the Blue Ridge Parkway.

Ferrum College
Ferrum, VA 24088

Facilities: Families are housed in air-conditioned 2-room suites, connected by bathrooms; swimming, hiking, tennis, horseback riding available

Notes: At present, summer accommodations are frequently booked for sports camps and conferences and are not available to individuals; however, they may be in the future, so contact the Director of Programs regarding availability of individual space

Telephone: 703-365-2121

Ferrum College, founded in 1913, is a liberal arts college affiliated with the Methodist Church. The 754-acre campus is located in a scenic rural area in the foothills of the Blue Ridge Mountains, 35 miles south of Roanoke.

Roanoke has a fine arts center, a transportation museum, and the Bain Dinner Theater. Within easy traveling distance of Ferrum are the Blue Ridge Parkway, Fairystone State Park, Mill Mountain, and the Booker T. Washington National Monument.

Eastern Mennonite College
Harrisonburg, VA 22801

Rooms available: May to mid-August (reservations essential)
Rates: $10 per person
Facilities: Cafeteria usually available, tennis, fitness trail
Policy on children: Accepted
Restrictions: No alcohol, no smoking in buildings
Telephone: 703-433-2771

Affiliated with the Mennonite Church, the College has a 106-acre campus in a rural area of the Shenandoah Valley about 2 miles from Harrisonburg, a town with 15,000 people. It is 120 miles from Richmond and Washington.

Of interest in the vicinity are Luray Caverns, New Market Civil War Museum and Battlefield, Lost River State Park, Skyline Drive, and Westover City Park.

Liberty University
Lynchburg, VA 24506

Rooms available: All year
Rates: $10 in advance, or $13 on arrival (higher in summer); no linens provided
Facilities: Snack bar, shared bathrooms
Policy on children: Accepted summer only
Restrictions: Visitors must have an educational purpose
Telephone: 804-582-2000

Liberty University is an independent Baptist institution founded in 1971. Its large campus is in an urban setting.

A city of 68,000 people, Lynchburg originally was laid out on some 45 acres of land owned by John Lynch. The Battle of Lynchburg was fought here in 1864, when an unsuccessful attempt was made to capture the stores held by the Confederate army. The city has several residential districts with mansions recalling its days as a successful tobacco town.

Sweet Briar College
Sweet Briar, VA 24595

Rooms available: All year
Rates: $41 single; $52.18 double

Facilities: Cafeteria, private bathrooms
Notes: Rooms are in Ellston Inn, a guest house on campus; there are campus theater projects, dances, art exhibits
Telephone: 804-381-6207

An independent college, Sweet Briar occupies 3,300 acres in a rural area about 12 miles from Lynchburg and 165 miles from Washington. There are a riding center and a swimming pool on campus, and some areas have been set aside for ecological studies. Despite its great size, the Sweet Briar campus is secluded in the foothills of the Blue Ridge Mountains.

Lynchburg, a city of 67,000, is the site of the 1864 Battle of Lynchburg and has several nineteenth-century residential districts, including Court House Hill.

WASHINGTON
The Evergreen State
state flower: western rhododendron; state bird: willow goldfinch

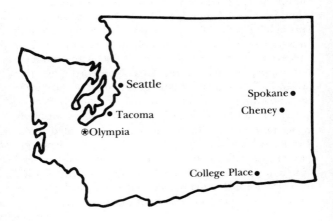

Washington was admitted to the Union as the forty-second state in 1889. Its state capital is Olympia, and its larger cities are Seattle, Spokane, and Tacoma. The coastal area west of the Cascade Mountains is wet, with moderate temperatures, while the eastern portion of the state is quite arid and is used primarily to raise livestock. Since Washington is a relatively treeless state except in the mountainous regions, irrigation is commonly used to raise apples, wheat, and hay. Aircraft and spacecraft are major products, with food ranking next. However, the state is perhaps best known for its national parks, islands, mountains, and seashore, which draw many visitors.

Seattle, located on Puget Sound, is a major seaport, as is Bellingham nearby. The Columbia River, which forms a boundary with Oregon, is used heavily for shipping and hydroelectric power for both states.

Eastern Washington University
Cheney, WA 99004

Rooms available: All year (reservations required)
Rates: $11 single; $9 per person, double
Facilities: Cafeteria, laundry, kitchenettes, both private and shared bathrooms, bookstore, swimming pool, most sports, theater during school year
Telephone: 509-359-7022

A publicly supported university, Eastern Washington was founded in 1882. The 335-acre campus is located 16 miles from Spokane. Cheney (population 7,600) is the site of Turnbull Wildlife Refuge, an important breeding ground for waterfowl, shorebirds, and upland game birds.

Spokane, with a population of 175,000, is an economic and cultural center for the area. Noteworthy are the Crosby Library and East Washington State Historical Society and Museum. In addition, the Museum of Native American Culture and St. John's Cathedral, an outstanding example of Gothic architecture, are located here. Riverfront Park, the site of Expo '74, features Japanese gardens, Canada Island, the Opera House and Convention Center, and an Imax theater with a screen five stories high. The locale has many lakes and is close to the mountains of Washington and northern Idaho.

Walla Walla College
College Place, WA 99324

Rooms available: June 6 to September 20 (reservations essential)
Rates: $15, dorm; $20, Whitman Lodge

Facilities: Cafeteria, laundry, kitchenettes, store, some private bathrooms, tennis, racquetball, weights, other sports
Policy on children: Accepted
Telephone: 509-527-2327

The College, which occupies 55 acres, was founded in 1894 by the Seventh-Day Adventist Church. It is located in the rolling hills and farms of southeastern Washington and is in the town of College Place, which has a population of about 6,000.

Walla Walla, which is nearby, has a population of 25,000 and two colleges. The presence of three colleges in such a small area means there are many cultural events. Visitors should see the Fort Walla Walla Museum complex, consisting of some fourteen buildings depicting pioneer life in the area.

Seattle Downtown YMCA
909 Fourth Avenue
Seattle, WA 98104

Rooms available: All year
Rates: $23 single; $27 double, including breakfast
Facilities: Shared bathrooms, fitness center, swimming pool
Notes: All-inclusive 2- to 5-day tours available, reasonably priced
Telephone: 206-382-5000

Far and away the largest city in Washington, Seattle has something to interest everyone. Located on a slip of land between mountains, lakes, and Puget Sound, Seattle's frequent rain serves to keep the city green and clean. Among the attractions of the city are some structures left over from a World's Fair, including a "space needle" that provides a view of the entire region. The expression "Skid Row" originated in Seattle as Skid Road, a road down which logs were rolled. Since the area is a leader in aircraft production, the Museum of Flight is well worth a visit, as are the Pioneer Square Historic District and Pike's Place Market.

WEST VIRGINIA
The Mountain State
state flower: rhododendron maximum; state bird: cardinal

The thirty-fifth state, West Virginia was admitted to the Union in 1863. Charleston is the capital, and Huntington, Wheeling, and Parkersburg are all large cities. The state is very hilly and is not known for its agriculture, even though some 60 percent of its population live in rural areas. It does raise a number of cash crops, especially tobacco, hay, and apples; however, manufacturing and coal mining are more important in the state's economy.

One of the most beautiful states in the nation because of its rolling terrain, West Virginia offers hunting, fishing, camping, and skiing, as well as the facilities of national parks like Harper's Ferry and White Sulphur Springs.

Marshall University
Huntington, WV 25701

Rooms available: Mid-May to mid-August (reservations required)

Rates: $10, single; $8 per person, double
Facilities: Cafeteria, laundry, store, shared bathrooms, tennis, swimming, racquetball
Policy on children: Accepted
Telephone: 304-696-3126

The University is a state-supported institution established in 1837. It occupies 45 acres in an urban area 50 miles from Charleston.

Named after Collis Huntington, then president of the Chesapeake and Ohio Railroad, Huntington has about 63,000 residents. It is primarily a manufacturing city, with the Ohio River on one side and a semicircle of hills around the rest. The city has an interesting civic center and the Heritage Museum, a restored railway yard with shops and restaurants located in old railway cars and warehouses. Tours of Pilgrim Glass, one of the local industries, are available.

West Virginia Institute of Technology
Montgomery, WV 25136

Rooms available: End of May to August 1 (reservations preferred)
Rates: Approximately $12 per person, plus linen charge
Facilities: Cafeteria, laundry, shared bathrooms, tennis, swimming, basketball
Telephone: 304-442-3183

Founded in 1895, this state-supported institution occupies 111 acres on a mountainside overlooking the small town of Montgomery and the Kanawha River. In the vicinity of Montgomery is Hawk's Nest State Park, with superb whitewater rafting and camping. Charleston, the nearest city, is 28 miles away.

Charleston (population 65,000) is the state capital. Daniel Boone lived across the river from Charleston from 1788 to 1795. Of interest are Coonskin Park, the Science and Cultural Center, and the state capitol, which is noted for its gold dome and rock-crystal chandelier.

College Accommodations

West Virginia University
Morgantown, WV 26506

Rooms available: Mid-May to second week in August
Rates: $22.50 single; $14 per person, double
Facilities: Cafeteria, sports facilities
Policy on children: Accepted
Notes: Visitors must have an educationally related purpose
Telephone: 304-293-2096

The University is a land-grant institution under state control. It was founded in 1867 and is located in Morgantown, a city of some 27,000 in the Scott's Run bituminous coalfield. It has a Personal Rapid Transit system, computer controlled and fully automated, which serves as a lab for engineering and urban-planning students.

Nearby are Coopers Rock State Park and the Seneca Glassworks. Seneca is one of the country's oldest firms producing a variety of fine glass objects, and tours of its operations should not be missed.

Salem College
Salem, WV 26426

Rooms available: Mid-May to mid-August
Rates: Approximately $8 per day per person, $45 per week
Facilities: Cafeteria, laundromat, shared bathrooms, kitchenettes, swimming pool
Policy on children: Accepted
Telephone: 304-782-5248

Salem College is a private institution founded in 1888. The 200-acre campus is located in a rural area 10 miles from Clarksburg. On campus is Fort New Salem, an outdoor museum featuring the arts and crafts of Appalachia.

Clarksburg (population 22,000) is famous as the birthplace of the Confederate general Stonewall Jackson. Nearby attractions include Canaan Valley, Blackwater Falls, Cheat Lake, and Tygart Lake.

Wheeling Jesuit College
Wheeling, WV 26003

Rooms available: Mid-May to mid-August (reservations required)

Rates: $25
Facilities: Cafeteria, laundry, store, shared bathrooms, gym, weight room, tennis, outdoor running track
Telephone: 304-243-2210

Wheeling Jesuit College occupies a 60-acre suburban campus some 60 miles from Pittsburgh, Pennsylvania.

Wheeling (population 63,000) is the site of the last battle of the American Revolution in 1782. The war had ended, but the news had not yet reached Wheeling!

The Capitol Music Hall in Wheeling attracts Saturday crowds for its country-and-western music, which is broadcast throughout the United States and Canada. Wheeling and Oglebay parks, the Good Zoo, the Mansion Museum, and West Virginia Independence Hall are among other local attractions. Country music aficionados are attracted to Jamboree in the Hills, a festival usually held in July.

College Accommodations

WISCONSIN
The Badger State
state flower: wood violet; state bird: robin

Wisconsin, "America's Dairyland," was admitted to the Union as the thirtieth state in 1848. Its capital is Madison, but Milwaukee is better known, especially for its beer, although the city does turn out diesel engines, metal products, and farm implements. Food processing is an important industry, with dairy products, especially cheese and butter, of primary importance.

With frontage on Lakes Superior and Michigan and a vast number of lakes and streams inland, Wisconsin is popular with fishermen and hunters. Tourists also enjoy the forty-nine state parks and national forests.

Viterbo College
La Crosse, WI 54601

Rooms available: Third week in May to August 1 (reservations essential)

Rates: From $15 for a private room, but variable according to type of accommodation (key deposit required)
Facilities: Cafeteria, laundry, kitchenettes, both private and shared bathrooms, tennis and other sports facilities
Policy on children: Accepted
Telephone: 608-784-0040 Ext. 358

Viterbo College was founded in 1931 and is a liberal arts college affiliated with the Catholic Church. Its campus occupies 5 acres in La Crosse, which is 140 miles from Minneapolis–St. Paul.

La Crosse has a population of about 50,000 and is located on the Mississippi at the junction of the Black and La Crosse rivers. Like Milwaukee, brewing is important, and the city also serves as a trading center for the area. The Pump House and Swarthout Museum are both worth a visit, while the Heileman Tourist Center offers free tours of the Heileman Brewery.

University of Wisconsin–Oshkosh
Oshkosh, WI 54901

Rooms available: All year
Rates: $12.25 single; $9.75 per person, double; $7.25 students
Facilities: Cafeteria, snack bars, shared bathrooms, bowling alleys, gym facilities, movies, live theater
Policy on children: Accepted
Telephone: 414-424-1121

Located on a 165-acre campus in the heart of the Fox River valley, the University of Wisconsin–Oshkosh was established in 1871.

Oshkosh (population 50,000) is ringed by two lakes and a river. Outdoor recreational activities available in the area include swimming, sailing, golf, tennis, fishing, and jogging. The International Fly-in, featuring antique, modern, and experimental airplanes, is held in Oshkosh the first week in August. The Paine Art Center and Arboretum and the Oshkosh Public Museum are attractive to visitors.

University of Wisconsin–Platteville
Platteville, WI 53818

Rooms available: Spring and summer (reservations preferred)
Rates: $7 single; $5 per person, double
Facilities: Cafeteria, par golf course, swimming, canoeing, campus Shakespeare Festival
Policy on children: Accepted
Restrictions: Visitors with business at the University preferred
Telephone: 608-342-1845

The University of Wisconsin–Platteville has a 360-acre campus of gently rolling land located in a rural area 25 miles from Dubuque, Iowa. A 90-acre recreation area is part of the main campus, and a 400-acre University farm is close by.

Platteville (population 9,600) was settled in 1827 following the discovery of lead and zinc nearby. The town was laid out by an English architect, and many features characteristic of Yorkshire are incorporated into its design. Cheese production now leads mining as the major industry of the area. A mining museum, the Rollo Jamison Museum, and Rowntree Stone Cottage are places of interest in the area.

George Williams College, Lake Geneva Campus
Williams Bay, WI 53191

Rooms available: All year
Rates: From $33 per room per night, varying according to season and type of accommodation; wide variety of accommodations includes rooms, suites, housekeeping cottages, lakefront villas, and lodges
Facilities: Cafeteria, laundry, shop, snack bar, private bathrooms, tennis, croquet, boating, skiing, swimming
Policy on children: Accepted
Restrictions: No pets; alcohol permitted in rooms only
Notes: Special programs available for seniors and families; farm tours and nature hikes possible
Telephone: 414-245-5531

Wisconsin

Located on 150 acres on the north shore of Lake Geneva at Williams Bay, George Williams College is about an hour's drive from Racine and Kenosha. In the general area are forty-nine parks, a zoo, the Yerkes Astronomical Observatory, Old Wisconsin, and the East Troy Trolley Museum.

Racine has a museum of fine arts and a historical museum. The Society for the Preservation and Encouragement of Barbershop Quartet Singing is located here, and there is a large library of Gay Nineties music. American Motors headquarters is also located here.

CANADA

The Dominion of Canada was established on July 1, 1867. Initially a British territory, Canada has retained many of its British roots, although it has been completely independent for many years. Canada has a population of around 25 million. The majority are of British stock, but there are people of all nationalities; for example, more Icelanders reside here than in Iceland. Most people live within 200 miles of the border with the United States, which is the longest undefended border in the world.

Canada shares many things with the United States, but it is definitely a foreign country. It has two official languages, French and English. The province of Quebec is primarily French speaking, as are several cities in the rest of the country.

Much of Canada is sparsely populated, but the cities offer high-quality cultural amenities: museums, theaters, ballet companies, symphony orchestras, fine restaurants, and elegant shopping areas. The remote areas of the country are unsurpassed for hunting, fishing, and other outdoor sports.

Since the rate of exchange is favorable to travelers from the United States, Canada is also a good place to visit and shop in, although smokers and drinkers will find their habits heavily taxed. Note that in order to drive your vehicle into Canada, you must have a copy of the vehicle registration and proof of insurance. This proof must take the form of a Canadian nonresident Inter-Provincial Motor Vehicle Liability Insurance Card, which is available from your insurance agent at no cost to you. You may find the road signs in Canada slightly confusing at first because they use the metric system; the number of kilometers times 6 (a kilometer is approximately six tenths of a mile) gives you the number of miles.

ALBERTA

Alberta has a population of about 2.5 million. Its capital is Edmonton. Calgary, in the southern part of the province, is known for the Winter Olympics held there recently and the annual Calgary Stampede.

The province has both the Rocky Mountains and rolling prairies. Of major interest in the Rockies are Banff and Jasper national parks, Lake Louise, and the Columbia Ice Field, which spawns several glaciers. Alberta is known for its oil and gas fields, and it also has very rich agricultural areas.

University of Calgary
Calgary, AB T2N 1N4

Rooms available: May through August (reservations required)
Rates: $15–$37 per person, including breakfast

University of Calgary (continued)

Facilities: Cafeteria, laundry, kitchenettes, store, both private and shared bathrooms, sports facilities, theater, lounges
Policy on children: Accepted
Notes: Pubs and restaurants are nearby
Telephone: 403-220-3210

The University of Calgary is a province-supported institution founded in 1945. It is affiliated with the Banff School of Fine Arts. It is located in the northwestern part of Calgary, a city of some 400,000 and location of the headquarters of many oil and gas companies. The University houses the athletes' village from the recent Winter Olympics, as well as the Nickel Art Museum and the Olympic Skating Oval.

Calgary's chinook winds give the city a relatively mild climate. The Calgary Stampede, begun in 1912, is always a sellout and is well worth seeing. In addition, the zoo, the planetarium, the Energeum, Heritage Park, Calgary Tower, and the Glenbow Museum are of interest. The city serves as a gateway to the Rockies, with Banff and Lake Louise about one and a half hours away.

University of Alberta
Edmonton, AB T6G 2H6

Rooms available: May through August (reservations preferred; front desk open 24 hours)
Rates: $21 single; $32 twin; lower student rates (major credit cards accepted)
Facilities: Cafeteria, laundry, store, some private bathrooms, sports facilities
Policy on children: Accepted
Restrictions: No pets, no smoking
Telephone: 403-492-4281

The University, founded in 1908, is a private school. The 154-acre campus is located on the North Saskatchewan River close to Edmonton.

Edmonton (population 500,000) has grown to its present standing as the capital of Alberta from a 1795 fur-trading post and 1895 Klondike gold rush boomtown; it has also enjoyed the oil boom of the 1970s. Of interest are the Alberta Natural Resources Science Center, Strathcona Archeological Center, and Polar Park, a reserve for animals from cold climates. First Edmonton Historical Park and Pioneer Village, the Ukrainian Museum, and the legislative buildings are other points of interest.

For ten days every July, Edmontonians parade the streets in Gay Nineties apparel, with nonconformists subject to citizen's arrest. The West Edmonton Mall is one of the largest in the world and offers many attractions. Weather in Edmonton is pleasant in summer, and the city is not far from the Rockies and Jasper National Park.

Fairview College
Fairview, AB T0H 1L0

Rooms available: May to August; limited openings the rest of the year (reservations required)
Rates: $15 per person
Facilities: Cafeteria, laundry, kitchenettes, some private bathrooms, gym, 3-hole golf course, lake, playing field
Policy on children: Accepted
Restrictions: No pets in rooms, no camping on campus
Telephone: 403-835-6652

Fairview, established in 1928, is located in the heart of the agriculturally rich Peace River district about 6 hours northwest of Edmonton. The College offers an equine pavilion, a demonstration apiary, a farm, a shooting range, and opportunities for camping, hunting, and fishing.

In addition to its agricultural richness, the area also has coal tars and oil-bearing sands that are of commercial importance. The scenic Rocky Mountains are only a few miles away, and summers in the north have days of extreme length that allow travelers to prolong their enjoyment.

College Accommodations

BRITISH COLUMBIA

Although British Columbia seems to be all mountains, its fertile valleys offer some of the best agricultural land in Canada. However, lumber is the leading industry, with tourism ranking second. The entire province is quite different geographically from the rest of Canada, and the train ride to Prince George gives the visitor a chance to appreciate this difference.

Canada's Pacific province was thought of for many years as the place where British expatriots and retirees settled. Although things have changed over the years, this image still adheres to Victoria, the capital. Located on Vancouver Island, Victoria is famous for the beauty of its gardens and parks. It gets much less rain than Vancouver, on the mainland. Frequent ferry service from Vancouver and Seattle makes Victoria easily accessible.

Vancouver is an extremely beautiful and cosmopolitan city. Its parks have very beautiful gardens, and its architecture is outstanding. The city's Asian population provides an exotic touch. Vancouver was the site of a recent World's Fair.

Simon Fraser University
Burnaby, BC V5A 1S6

Rooms available: May to third week in August (reservations required)
Rates: $17–$26 per person (suites with private baths available at higher rates)
Facilities: Cafeteria, kitchens, laundry, lounge, store, shared bathrooms, gymnasium, pool, track, trails, museum on campus
Policy on children: Accepted
Restrictions: No pets
Telephone: 604-291-4201 or 4503

One of the newer universities in Canada, Simon Fraser is located about 10 miles from downtown Vancouver in a quiet mountain setting. The campus was designed by Arthur Erickson, who designed many public buildings in Canada and is now involved in some of the reconstruction of downtown Los Angeles. The design of the campus is still controversial, although it is now over 30 years old. The situation atop Burnaby Mountain is imposing, and a huge atrium is the centerpiece of the construction.

University of British Columbia
Vancouver, BC V6T 1W2

Rooms available: First week in May to third week in August
Rates: Variable, depending on type of accommodation; an apartment with private bathroom costs from $25 to $50
Facilities: Cafeteria, restaurant, kitchenettes, laundry, stores, both private and shared bathrooms, living rooms in suites
Policy on children: Accepted
Telephone: 604-228-5441 or 2963

The University was established in 1908 as a provincially supported school. It is located on the Point Grey Peninsula in the city of Vancouver and occupies a campus of 1,000 acres. The University's Museum of Anthropology is memorable, as are its botanical gardens.

Vancouver has many attractions, among them Stanley and Queen Elizabeth parks. Although Expo is long gone, its site still offers a magnificent location, central to almost every area of the city. British Columbia Place Stadium, the

College Accommodations

University of British Columbia (continued)

planetarium, the Gaslight district, Granville Island and its market, and the many shops and restaurants make the city a delight to visit.

Vancouver has a large Oriental enclave. Van Dusen Botanical Gardens is enjoyable, and the North Shore Museum juxtaposes a modern building with the ancient artifacts within.

University of Victoria
Victoria, BC V8W 2Y2

Rooms available: May 1 to end of August (reservations preferred)
Rates: $20 single; $32 double, including breakfast
Facilities: Cafeteria, laundry, store, gym, pool, sports facilities
Policy on children: Accepted
Telephone: 604-721-8395

The University's 380-acre campus is located about 5 miles from the city of Victoria.

Victoria is known to be "more English than England." It is a small, slow-paced city with no industry to speak of, catering to the provincial government, retired folk, and the University. Nevertheless, it is a favorite of tourists, and high tea at the Empress Hotel on the harbor is not to be missed. Butchart Gardens is spectacular, as are the parks and beaches.

A large island with less rain than Vancouver, Victoria is well worth exploring. There are many ferry links to the mainland, including Seattle, and all ferries take motor vehicles.

MANITOBA

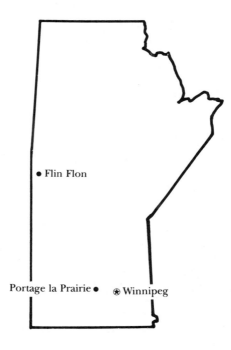

Manitoba became a province in 1870. Its capital is Winnipeg, a city of some 650,000 people located at the junction of the Red and Assiniboine rivers.

One of the prairie provinces, Manitoba nevertheless is distinguished by its ocean port on Hudson Bay in the north. Both grain and cattle are shipped to many parts of the world when this port is ice free. Although Manitoba was initially an agricultural province, manufacturing, especially of garments, now makes up about half of the economy. Lakes and forest abound, so water sports, fishing, and hunting are excellent.

Manitoba is probably one of Canada's most culturally diverse provinces. It numbers among its population many Icelanders, as well as Ukrainians, Jews, Germans, Italians, Indians, and French. People of British heritage are well represented, with the city of Selkirk having been established by Lord Selkirk, a Scottish nobleman.

University of Manitoba
Winnipeg, MB R3T 2N2

Rooms available: May to August (reservations required)
Rates: Approximately $12 per person (call for exact prices)
Facilities: Cafeteria, laundry, store, shared bathrooms, sports facilities
Policy on children: Accepted, under adult supervision
Telephone: 204-474-9717

The University, founded in 1877, is a provincially funded institution. Its 685-acre campus is located in Ft. Garry, some 7 miles from the heart of Winnipeg.

Winnipeg is a metropolitan city, with the parliament buildings, the Museum of Man and Nature, an art gallery, Assiniboine Park and Zoo, and the Pan Am Pool among its attractions. Although this city of 650,000 is somewhat isolated, the performing arts are well represented and include the Royal Winnipeg Ballet, an opera company, and a symphony orchestra. The outdoor theater in Kildonan Park stages musicals in summer. An ethnic festival is held each summer, as is an Icelandic celebration in nearby Gimli, a fishing village and resort that is home to a large Icelandic population. Winnipeg adjoins the smaller St. Boniface, a French-speaking city, providing an example of the diversity that is peculiarly Canadian.

NEW BRUNSWICK

Named after the house of Brunswick from which England's rulers came at the time of its founding, New Brunswick is the largest and most westerly of the maritime provinces. It is surrounded by water on three sides, and its boundary with the state of Maine on the fourth side was not fixed until 1842.

New Brunswick is mainly rural, with its largest city and capital at Fredericton. Passamaquoddy Bay and the town of St. John are located at the head of the Bay of Fundy, which has tides reaching 50 feet in height. The "tidal bore" at the mouth of the Saint John River, where the waters reverse and flow upstream, is a popular tourist attraction. Campobello Island, summer home of President Franklin D. Roosevelt, is in New Brunswick.

Given the huge forests of New Brunswick, lumbering and papermaking are major industries. New Brunswick seed potatoes are important, while tourism and fishing are also major industries.

University of New Brunswick
Fredericton, NB E3B 5A3

Rooms available: Mid-May to third week in August
Rates: $22 single; $32 twin

College Accommodations

University of New Brunswick (continued)
Facilities: Cafeteria, laundry, store, shared bathrooms, tennis, squash, swimming
Policy on children: Accepted
Telephone: 506-453-4891

The University of New Brunswick moved to its present location in the center of Loyalist country in 1829. The campus is centrally located only a few minutes from the downtown area.

Fredericton (population 44,000) is the capital of New Brunswick and stands on the site of an old French village known as St. Annes. It obtained its present-day name in 1785 from Loyalists departing the young United States who wanted to honor King George by naming their new city after his second son, Frederick. Of interest in the city are the Antique Arms Museum, Beaverbrook Art Gallery, the CFB Gagetown Military Museum, and Christ Church Cathedral.

NEWFOUNDLAND

Newfoundland, which includes Labrador, is Canada's newest province. However, it is the oldest in terms of European settlement, since it is closest to Europe and was visited throughout the centuries by European fishermen, prominent among whom were the Portuguese. Fishing is still the dominant industry in Newfoundland, and sport fishing is very popular, because the cold waters encourage the growth of very big tuna, swordfish, and other desirable species.

World War II veterans may recall Gander and Goose Bay as the locations of extremely large airfields on the island of Newfoundland and on Labrador, respectively. These are still in use, primarily as emergency airfields for transatlantic flights.

Despite the great age of its settlements, Newfoundland is an impoverished, sparsely populated province that is only now beginning to take advantage of its many natural resources. There is frequent ferry and air service to the mainland.

Memorial University of Newfoundland
St. John's, NF A1C 5S7

Rooms available: Second week of May to third week of August (reservations required)
Rates: $12 students; $16 nonstudents
Facilities: Cafeterias, dining halls, laundry, shared bathrooms, aquarena, tennis courts
Policy on children: Accepted
Telephone: 709-737-7590 or 9592

Memorial University was founded in 1925 and is located in the oldest city of North America, St. John's. With a population of 85,000, St. John's is the capital, principal port, and main commercial center on the island. The Colonial Buildings, seat of government from 1850 to 1860, house provincial archives. The Regatta, held the first weekend of August, has been in existence longer than any other organized sporting event in North America; it dates back to 1826.

St. John's became important because it is closer to Europe than any other North American city. The Anglican Cathedral, a fine example of ecclesiastical Gothic architecture; the Basilica of St. John the Baptist, built in the shape of a Latin cross; and the old Garrison Church are all worth seeing.

College Accommodations

NOVA SCOTIA

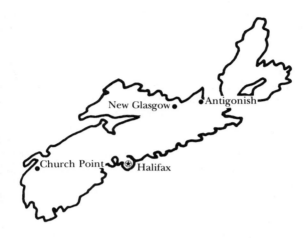

Another of Canada's maritime provinces, Nova Scotia was so named because the country reminded early settlers of their Scottish homeland. This Scottish influence remains, although there are many French-speaking Acadians living there. The forefathers of today's Louisiana Cajuns fled from Nova Scotia to the United States.

Nova Scotia is almost completely surrounded by water, and, as a result, fishing is of great importance in the economy. Mineral wealth is substantial and is only now being exploited, while tourism is slowly coming into its own. Naturally, all forms of water sports are popular, as are hunting and camping.

The capital at Halifax has a reconstructed waterfront and a port known to many veterans. Sydney, on Cape Breton Island, has coal mines extending miles under the Atlantic. Peggy's Cove, a quaint fishing village, is worth seeing, as is the museum at Baddeck, home of Alexander Graham Bell, inventor of the telephone. This modern museum gives an idea of the breadth of Bell's interests.

There is frequent ferry and airplane service from the United States, as well as from other parts of Canada, and the drive around Cape Breton on the Cabot Trail is especially charming.

Nova Scotia

St. Francis Xavier University
Antigonish, NS B2G 1C0

Rooms available: May 15 to August 15, on a space-available basis
Rates: $15 single; $13 per person, double
Facilities: Cafeteria open weekdays and certain other times, swimming pool, tennis courts
Policy on children: Accepted
Notes: Clarke Observatory is located on campus
Telephone: 902-867-3970 (Conference Office)

St. Francis Xavier University was founded in 1853. Its hallmark has been service to the community since the early days of the Antigonish Movement, a program of self-help for farmers and fishermen in the area that included pioneering work in the fields of credit unions and cooperatives. It continues in that tradition.

Antigonish is located in northeastern Nova Scotia, midway between Halifax and Sydney on the Trans-Canada Highway. Prince Edward Island, the beaches of George Bay, and fishing villages are all close by.

Université Sainte-Anne
Church Point, NS B0W 1M0

Rooms available: All year except for the period July 1 to August 15 (reservations required)
Rates: $13 students; $15.50 nonstudents
Facilities: Cafeteria, swimming pool, gym, library
Policy on children: Accepted
Telephone: 902-769-2114

Université Sainte-Anne is a small university located in a quiet rural setting on the shores of St. Mary's Bay in Digby County. Its main goal is to respond to the cultural, social, and economic needs of the Acadians in the province.

Of interest to visitors are Mavilette Beach, arts and crafts shops, churches, fisheries, festivals, and the local parks. Digby, a nearby town with a population of 2,600, is famous for its "Digby chicken" and smoked salmon. It is the home of one of the largest scallop fleets in the world.

College Accommodations

Dalhousie University
Halifax, NS B3H 4J2

Rooms available: Mid-May to mid-August (reservations and deposit required)
Rates: $24 single; $33.50 double, including breakfast
Facilities: Cafeteria, shared bathrooms, fitness center (available at $3 per day)
Policy on children: Accepted
Telephone: 902-424-8840

Dalhousie is the largest and one of the oldest schools in Atlantic Canada, having been founded in 1818. The campus occupies more than 60 acres in a central residential area of Halifax.

Halifax (population 115,000) is the capital of Nova Scotia and has one of the finest harbors in the world. The city has numerous museums, parks, and historic landmarks. Noteworthy are the Chapel of Our Lady of Sorrows, Government House, Halifax Citadel National Park, and the Nova Scotia Museum. Peggy's Cove, an artists' colony, is within driving distance.

Mount Saint Vincent University
Halifax, NS B3M 2J6

Rooms available: Mid-May to mid-August (reservations preferred)
Rates: $19 single; $27 double
Facilities: Cafeteria, laundry, kitchenettes, store, shared bathrooms, game room, gym, exercise room
Policy on children: Accepted
Restrictions: No pets
Notes: Dinner theater available during June and July
Telephone: 902-443-4450

Mount St. Vincent University was established in 1873 by the Sisters of Charity of St. Vincent de Paul as the only independent women's college in the British Commonwealth. It is located on 52 acres overlooking historic Bedford Basin in Halifax. There is an art gallery on campus.

ONTARIO

Located in the center of Canada, Ontario is one of the country's most populous provinces, as well as one of its most prosperous ones. It fronts on four of the Great Lakes and offers a view of Niagara Falls unavailable on the American side. The Niagara Peninsula is considered Canada's "Banana Belt," with many fruit trees and even tobacco grown there.

The Shaw and Shakespeare festivals are held on the Niagara Peninsula each year. Cosmopolitan Toronto and Ottawa, the capital of Canada, offer a degree of cultural diversity unequaled by many other cities.

Northern Ontario supports mining and lumbering on a large scale, and there are opportunities for fishing, water sports, and hunting throughout the province. Agriculture is very important in the economy of the province, and almost half of all the goods manufactured in Canada come from Ontario.

University of Guelph
Guelph, ON N1G 2W1

Rooms available: Third week in April to third week in August (reservations required)
Rates: $20 single; $13.50 per person, double
Facilities: Cafeteria, laundry, kitchenettes, store, shared bathrooms

University of Guelph (continued)
Policy on children: Accepted
Notes: The campus is in a rural area with jogging trails
Telephone: 519-824-4120

The University was founded in 1964 and includes the Ontario Agricultural College.

A city of about 60,000, Guelph was founded in 1827 by John Galt, a Scottish novelist. It is located in southern Ontario, about 45 miles west of Toronto, and is an industrial city located in a rich agricultural area. Tobacco is grown in the area, and electrical items and agricultural machinery are among its major products. There are many historic sites in Guelph and nearby Niagara Falls. The Shaw Festival at Niagara on the Lake and the Shakespeare Festival at Stratford are special events.

University of Western Ontario
London, ON N6A 3K7

Rooms available: May through August (reservations required)
Rates: $20 adults, $15 students (including alumni and senior citizens); these rates are for bed and breakfast
Facilities: Cafeteria, laundry, kitchenettes, store, shared bathrooms, tennis, squash, swimming, weight room
Policy on children: Accepted if over 12
Telephone: 519-672-5461

The University of Western Ontario was chartered in 1878 and is a public institution. The 408-acre campus is located on the banks of the Thames River, some 2 hours east of Detroit and 2 hours west of Toronto.

London, Ontario, with a population of about 260,000, broadcasts its ties to its namesake in England in the name of its river and in street names like Piccadilly, Oxford Street, and Pall Mall. The city is an important commercial and industrial center, with a great number of parks. This, coupled with the century-old custom of planting a thousand trees each year, has earned London the nickname of "Forest City."

Of particular interest in London are the Centennial Museum, historic Elden House, the London Regional Art Gallery, and Labatt's Pioneer Brewery, which has been restored to its original nineteenth-century appearance.

London is a 40-minute drive from Stratford and its Shakespeare Festival.

York University
North York, ON M3J 1P3

Rooms available: Third week in May to third week in August (reservations required)
Rates: $29 adults, $14.25 students
Facilities: Cafeteria, laundry, store, shared bathrooms, tennis, squash, swimming
Policy on children: Accepted
Notes: Metropolitan Toronto Track and Field Center is on campus
Telephone: 416-736-5020

York University, founded in 1959, is a provincially supported school located on 570 acres a half hour's drive from downtown Toronto. Black Creek Pioneer Village is nearby, as are the many museums, theaters, and restaurants of Toronto.

Carleton University
Ottawa, ON K1S 5B6

Rooms available: Early May to late August
Rates: $25 single; $19 per person, double (including breakfast)
Facilities: Cafeteria, pub, laundry, store, shared bathrooms, swimming pool, squash, tennis, indoor track, fitness center
Policy on children: Accepted
Notes: Scenic walks and jogging tracks on campus
Telephone: 613-788-5609

Carleton University occupies 152 picturesque acres between the Rideau River and the Rideau Canal in Canada's capital. Ottawa, a graceful city of 300,000, is noted for its bicycle paths, flower gardens, and the Changing of the Guard at the capitol building.

The city was chosen as the capital by Queen Victoria in 1857, and today it is steeped in a grace and elegance that are epitomized by the Parliament buildings. Ottawa's residents have the luxury of living in a parklike setting and

Carleton University (continued)

nonindustrial environment while benefiting from the cultural life and pageantry unique to a capital city. Visitors should be sure to see the new National Gallery and the Museum of Science and Industry.

Brock University
St. Catharines, ON L2S 3A1

Rooms available: May 1 to September 1
Rates: $22.50 single; $18.50 per person, double
Facilities: Laundry, pub, shared bathrooms, pool, athletic facilities, theater
Policy on children: Accepted
Telephone: 416-688-5392

Brock is located in St. Catharines at the edge of the Niagara Escarpment. The city has a population of about 125,000, and the University encompasses some 540 acres of the most inviting woodlands and trails in the area. It is minutes away from Niagara Falls, the Welland Canal, and the vineyards of the Canadian fruit belt.

St. Catharines, 75 miles from Toronto and 30 miles from Buffalo, is the site of the annual Shaw Festival. It has a historical museum and Tivoli Miniature World, a collection of replicas of the world's major structures. The surrounding area is especially beautiful during Blossom Week in early May. A lookout platform at Lock 3 of the Welland Canal gives a view of ships on the St. Lawrence Seaway.

Confederation College
Thunder Bay, ON P7C 4W1

Rooms available: May to mid-August (reservations required)
Rates: Variable, depending on length of stay; a double room would cost $70 for a week
Facilities: Cafeteria, laundry, kitchenettes, store, some private bathrooms, fitness center
Policy on children: Accepted
Notes: Golf course nearby; library and National Exhibition Center on campus
Telephone: 807-475-6381

Confederation College is centrally located in an urban area of Thunder Bay on the north shore of Lake Superior.

The city of Thunder Bay was established in 1969 by the merger of Fort William and Port Arthur, bringing the total population to around 112,000. It is the third-largest port in Canada, with storage facilities for 105 million bushels of grain. The various ethnic groups of which Canada is composed are recognized in the International Friendship Garden. Mount McKay, on the Ojibway Indian Reservation, offers an excellent view of the area. Also of interest to visitors are Old Fort William, a reconstruction of the original fort; various parks; Kakebeka Falls; and an active amethyst mine with samples for sale.

University of Toronto
Toronto, ON M5S 1A1

Rooms available: Mid-May to end of August (reservations required)
Rates: $35 single; $23 per person, double; children $20, including supervision (all rates include breakfast and daily maid service)
Facilities: Cafeteria open on weekdays, laundry, shared bathrooms, athletic facilities
Policy on children: Those over 5 accepted
Telephone: 416-978-8735

The University was founded as a provincially supported school in 1827. Its main campus is located on a spacious site in downtown Toronto.

Toronto is a metropolitan city of 2 million people noted for its excellent public transportation, its shops and boutiques, and its galleries and museums. Worth a visit are the Art Gallery of Ontario, the Royal Ontario Museum, and the Parliament buildings. Historic sites include Casa Loma and Fort York, while Canada's Wonderland, a theme park, and Centario Place, an exhibition center, are also of interest. City Hall, Nathan Phillips Square, and the O'Keefe Center offer impressive architecture; the CN Tower is the largest free-standing structure in the world. Visitors also enjoy the Great Toronto Adventure, a light show using sixty projectors.

College Accommodations

University of Waterloo
Waterloo, ON N2J 4C1

Rooms available: May to end of August
Rates: Variable, depending on type of accommodation, but moderate
Facilities: Cafeteria, dining rooms, laundry facilities, kitchenettes, store, shared bathrooms, swimming pool, sports
Policy on children: Accepted
Notes: Golf course, galleries, and museum on campus
Telephone: 519-884-4072

The University of Waterloo was founded in 1957 as a publicly supported institution. The 1,000-acre campus is located in Waterloo, twin city of Kitchener, with a combined population of around 170,000.

Most of the settlers in the area were of German Mennonite origin and came to Ontario from Pennsylvania. Their descendants are still in evidence in rural areas of the Grand River Valley and can be seen at the Wednesday and Saturday markets.

Doon Pioneer Village is a re-creation of an early Canadian village. Woodside National Historic Park contains the boyhood home of former prime minister William Lyon Mackenzie King, restored to its nineteenth-century appearance. This is festival country, and the Shakespeare Festival is held annually at nearby Stratford.

Wilfrid Laurier University
Waterloo, ON N2L 3C5

Rooms available: Mid-May to mid-August
Rates: Call for current rates
Facilities: Cafeteria, shared bathrooms, Olympic-size pool, tennis courts
Policy on children: Accepted
Telephone: 519-884-1970

This University is named for a former prime minister of Canada. It is located in an agricultural region where fruits, vegetables, and grapes are grown. The campus is six blocks from downtown Waterloo, where a Mennonite farmers' market is held regularly during the summer months.

University of Windsor
Windsor, ON N9B 3P4

Rooms available: Mid-May to third week in August (reservations preferred)
Rates: $22 single; $18 per person, double
Facilities: Cafeteria, kitchenettes, store, shared bathrooms, swimming pool, facilities for most sports
Policy on children: Accepted
Telephone: 519-252-4232

The University of Windsor was founded as Assumption College in 1857 and achieved university status in 1953. It has an attractive location near the Detroit River and the entrance to the Ambassador Bridge to Detroit.

Windsor (population 200,000) is an ocean port of entry as well as an inland one, and it is also an important industrial center. Of interest to visitors are Ouellette Avenue Mall, the tropical gardens, a waterfront park, Point Pelee National Park, the Jack Miner Bird Sanctuary, and Fort Walden Historical Park.

PRINCE EDWARD ISLAND

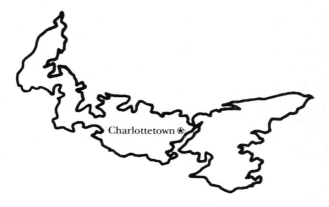

Canada's smallest province is located in the Gulf of St. Lawrence just north of New Brunswick and Nova Scotia. It was named for Prince Edward, Duke of Kent, in 1799. This large, relatively treeless island is noted for being the home of Lucy Maud Montgomery, author of *Anne of Green Gables,* and for the potatoes that flourish in its red, iron-rich soil.

Charlottetown, with its large harbor, is the capital and largest city of the island.

Fishing is quite important on the island, as is agriculture. The various beaches and national parks are increasing in popularity, and tourists will find driving around the island quite easy, even though it is about 140 miles long and 30 miles wide at its greatest. Frequent car ferries connect the island to the mainland.

University of Prince Edward Island
Charlottetown, PE C1A 4P3

Rooms available: Third week in May to mid-August
Rates: $18.95 for rooms, $42 for apartments (2 bedrooms, bath, kitchenette; limit 5 people), including breakfast
Facilities: Cafeteria open July and August, laundry facilities
Policy on children: Accepted
Notes: Planetarium on campus
Telephone: 902-566-0442

The University is located in the provincial capital of Charlottetown (population 20,000).

Charlottetown is a small city that is comfortable for walking in. It is a commercial and educational center that in many ways still evokes the feeling of a colonial seaport. Old Charlottetown, a restored waterfront area, houses craft shops, boutiques, and restaurants. The Charlottetown Festival, held at the Confederation Center of the Arts from mid-June to mid-September, features the original Canadian Musical Theater and gallery presentations. Beaconsfield is a Victorian-style house with displays of provincial artifacts.

QUEBEC

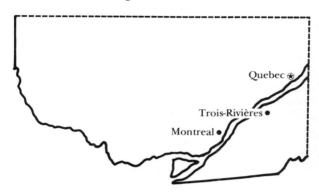

Known as "la Belle Province," Quebec shows its French heritage in many ways. The French language predominates, although many residents are bilingual. The Roman Catholic Church is dominant.

Montreal is the largest city in Canada, and this cosmopolitan center has much to offer the visitor, including French cuisine. Quebec City, the provincial capital, gives a historical view of Canada.

Natural resources are of great importance in the province, and it exports much of its hydroelectric power to the United States. Fishing is a major industry, while agriculture ranks third in the economy. Opportunities for water sports, sport fishing, and hunting are unexcelled.

McGill University
Montreal, PQ H3A 2B4

Rooms available: Mid-May to mid-August
Rates: $28 adults, $21 students (weekly rates available; deposit required)
Facilities: Cafeteria and box lunches available, laundry, kitchenettes, shared bathrooms, athletic facilities (available at nominal fee)
Policy on children: Accepted
Telephone: 514-398 6367

McGill, a private institution, was founded in 1821. It is one of the oldest and finest schools in Canada. The 80-acre

McGill University (continued)

campus is located on the slope of Mount Royal in the center of Montreal and is convenient to shops, museums, and other places of interest.

Two thirds of Montreal's over 1 million residents are French speaking, and the French atmosphere is strong. There is a blend of genteel culture, haute cuisine, and old-world customs, all in a modern, North American environment.

Montreal has an underground city that is lined with shops, cafes, and fine restaurants and is connected with buildings on the surface. About 10 minutes from the downtown area, Terre des Hommes uses some of the old Expo buildings to form an amusement park and exhibition pavilions. Old Montreal is a restored area that houses museums, artisans, and restaurants. Among many other items of interest are the Railway Museum, the McCord Museum, the Basilica of Notre Dame de Montréal, Christ Church Cathedral, the Montreal Museum of Fine Arts, and the Musée des Arts Décoratifs de Montréal.

Université de Montreal
Montreal, PQ H3C 3J7

Rooms available: Beginning of May to third week in August (reservations required)
Rates: $17 students; $27 nonstudents
Facilities: Cafeteria, laundry, shared bathrooms, tennis, racquetball
Policy on children: Not accepted
Notes: The Metro station is a 5-minute walk, and downtown Montreal is a 20-minute subway ride away
Telephone: 514-343-6531

This is a French-speaking school established in 1876 as a branch of Université Laval. It became autonomous in 1919. The campus is located on Mount Royal, an ideal place to enjoy a lovely, quiet environment. St. Joseph's Shrine is a nearby attraction.

Université Laval
Quebec City, PQ G1K 7P4

Rooms available: Mid-May to third week in August
Rates: $15–$25
Facilities: Cafeteria, laundry, store, shared bathrooms, facilities for most sports
Restrictions: No pets; no credit cards accepted
Notes: Geological and botanical gardens on campus
Telephone: 418-656-2921

Laval is one of the oldest universities, and the oldest French-language one, in the Americas. The University occupies a 500-acre site in the St. Foy area, 4 kilometers west of Quebec City.

Quebec, a city of about 170,000, has a strategic location on the St. Lawrence River, with bluffs rising some 300 feet above the river. Upper Town was built on the heights, while Lower Town, the mercantile center of the city during the turbulent French-English battles that lasted until 1793, was built on the river flats. Lower Town has seventeenth-century buildings, while Upper Town has modern ones.

Quebec is French in language, spirit, and culture. It is the only walled city in the Americas outside of Mexico. Sightseeing includes the Château Frontenac hotel, the Citadel, the Musée d'Aire, the Musée du Fort, the Musée du Québec, Place Royale, the Ramparts, and the Parliament buildings. Nearby are Montmorency Falls and Park and Île d'Orléans, with its French atmosphere and old crafts.

Université du Québec à Trois-Rivières
Trois-Rivières, PQ G9A 5H7

Rooms available: Mid-May to mid-August (reservations required)
Rates: $20 per day; $60 per week; $195 per month
Facilities: Cafeteria, laundry, kitchenettes, store, private bathrooms
Policy on children: Accepted
Telephone: 819-378-0385

Université du Québec à Trois-Rivières (continued)

This is a province-supported coeducational university. It was founded in 1969 and is in a city setting with easy access to Montreal.

The second-oldest city in the province, Trois-Rivières was founded in 1634. Located midway between Quebec City and Montreal, it is named for the three channels of the St. Maurice River at its junction with the St. Lawrence. The old section of the city is renowned for its eighteenth-century structures, especially the renovated Manoir de Tonnacour, built in 1723 and now housing a contemporary art gallery.

Les Forges du St. Maurice National Park is the site of the first iron-making forge in Canada and offers a glimpse of times past. While there are a number of churches of interest, the Ursuline Monastery of 1697 is particularly memorable and houses a museum and art collection.

SASKATCHEWAN

Known among Canadians as a flat province given over to farming, Saskatchewan nevertheless has much to offer sightseers. Its capital at Regina was the headquarters of the Northwest Mounted Police, now the Royal Canadian Mounted Police, who still maintain a facility here to train horses and riders for the famous musical ride. Regina was so named by Princess Louise, daughter of Queen Victoria, in honor of her mother.

Site of almost half of Canada's improved farmlands, Saskatchewan is definitely a prairie province and has farms that seem to extend for miles. Potash is mined in the province, and oil and gas are rapidly becoming important revenue producers, as are other minerals such as sodium sulphate.

University of Regina
Regina, SK S4S 0A2

Rooms available: May to mid-August
Rates: $25 single; $18 per person, double
Facilities: Kitchen, laundry, TV lounges, sports facilities
Telephone: 306-584-4777

Founded in 1974, the University of Regina is a province-supported coeducational institution. Its 330-acre campus is in a city setting in Regina.

Regina is located in the heart of one of the world's great wheat-growing areas. Although Saskatchewan is largely flat and treeless, Regina is built around a large park and lake.

MORE OUTSTANDING TITLES FROM PETERSON'S

NEW EDITION

LEARNING VACATIONS®

Gerson G. Eisenberg

Learning Vacations® is a treasure trove of enriching vacation opportunities. The new edition of this bestselling travel guide covers 500 programs for every interest, age, and budget—making it the perfect resource for anyone who is tired of a routine vacation and looking for something new.

Learning Vacations® describes a wide variety of mind-expanding activities such as:

- Art tours of Europe
- Whale-watching trips off Baja California
- Gourmet cooking courses
- African safaris
- Writing seminars
- Mountain climbing
- Photography workshops
- Archaeological digs
- River rafting trips
- Music and dance festivals

Each description in *Learning Vacations®* gives full details on:

- Program content
- Duration
- Accommodations
- Costs
- Whom to contact for more information
- Sponsoring organization
- Qualifications of instructors

"Our nation's finest travel book."
Arthur Frommer

$11.95 paperback

NEW EDITION

PETERSON'S SUMMER OPPORTUNITIES FOR KIDS AND TEENAGERS 1990

Published to provide a year-round resource for families of the 4 million young people who participate in summer activities each year, this guide covers more than 1,200 summer programs.

Programs in the guide offer activities that range from art and aerospace engineering to rafting and writing and include those offered by private schools, colleges, camps, religious organizations, and travel and sports groups.

A new easy-to-scan chart has been added to help readers quickly identify the programs that provide the activities they seek. Complete profiles on each program include:

- Location of the program
- Program offerings
- Participants for whom the program is designed
- Program costs
- Jobs available to high school and college students
- Availability of financial aid

". . . most readable and informative"
Changing Times

$16.95 paperback
$32.95 hardcover

Look for these and other Peterson's titles in your local bookstore